CULTURE SMART!

# CHINA

Kathy Flower

Graphic Arts Books

First published in Great Britain 2003
by Kuperard, an imprint of Bravo Ltd.

Series Editor  Geoffrey Chesler
Design  DW Design

Simultaneously published in the U.S.A. and Canada
by Graphic Arts Center Publishing Company
P. O. Box 10306, Portland, OR 97296-0306

Third printing 2005

Library of Congress Cataloging-in-Publication Data

Flower, Kathy.
China : a quick guide to customs and etiquette / Kathy Flower.
    p. cm. — (Culture smart!)
Includes bibliographical references and index.
ISBN 1-55868-702-5 (alk. paper)
1. China—Civilization. 2. China—Social life and customs. I.
Quick guide to customs and etiquette. II. Title. III. Series.
DS721.F583 2003
951—dc21

                                    2002015668

Printed in Hong Kong

Cover image: View over the Summer Palace, Beijing.
*Travel Ink/Abbie Enock*

**CultureShock!**Consulting and **Culture Smart!** guides both cont
to and regularly feature in the weekly travel program "Fast 
on BBC World TV.

## About the Author

KATHY FLOWER is a radio and television producer, scriptwriter, and trainer who has specialized in the teaching of English as a Foreign Language. After training teachers for the British Council in Paris, she worked in Beijing from 1981 to 1983 and presented China's first major English-language teaching series, "Follow Me," on Chinese TV. She is still known to millions of viewers as *laoshi*, or "teacher." She has returned to China many times and now works for the BBC World Service.

## Other Books in the Series

Other titles are in p‌‍                    ‍    ‍
contact: info@kup‍

The publishers would like to thank **CultureShock!**Consulting for its help in researching and developing the concept for this series.

# contents

# contents

# Map of China

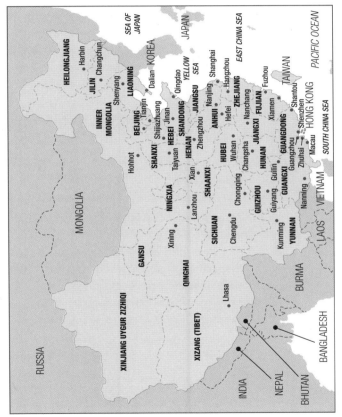

# introduction

For thousands of years, the Chinese believed
that they had created a perfect social system.
Dynasties came and went, but China and its
"Chineseness" remained essentially unchanged
until the twentieth century. The last one
hundred years, however, have seen China
embrace every possible form of social
organization and undergo enormous political
and economic change, at an often terrible price.
But as the new millennium dawns, China seems
set to join the rest of the world as an emerging
superpower, and a force for good in the
world community.

China is at last harnessing, rather than
repressing, the talents of its intelligent,
entrepreneurial, and hardworking people to
create prosperity and stability. The old guard of
conservative, uneducated officials, who had
acquired their jobs through Party connections
rather than merit, has given way to a younger
generation of highly educated, charismatic men
and, increasingly, women, who are questioning,
challenging, and eager to absorb new ideas.

The Chinese are proud of the achievements of
their country, and of the considerable influence
of their ancient civilization, but this pride is no
longer tainted by the xenophobia of old. Indeed,
the irony of the Cultural Revolution was that

Mao Zedong and his mobs of Red Guards not only regarded most foreigners as spies, but also attempted to destroy every value that the Chinese had traditionally held dear: family, education, respect for the elderly, loyalty to superiors, traditional festivals, thousands of books, antique scrolls and paintings, statues, and other art treasures. Those days are well and truly over now, and the Chinese people are free to enjoy the best of their traditions along with the benefits of modern life.

*Culture Smart! China* is a "good guest's guide" for the visitor who would like to learn a little more about the distinctive traditions, sensibilities, and modern way of life of the 1.2 billion people who live in China. It explains deep-seated attitudes, and describes the social, economic, and cultural changes that are taking place. It dispels some common Western misconceptions, and gives practical advice on what to expect and how to behave in unfamiliar social situations. Whether you are visiting on business or for pleasure, we hope it will enable you to discover for yourself the warmth, complexity, and vast potential of this fascinating and important country.

I would like to dedicate this book to my friends in China.                    KF

# Key Facts

| Official Name | The People's Republic of China (PRC); in Mandarin, *Zhonghua Renmin Gonghe Guo.* | The island of Taiwan (which has its own government) is called the Republic of China. |
| --- | --- | --- |
| Capital City | Beijing (Peking) | |
| Main Cities | Chongqing (Chungking), Shenyang (Mukden), Wuhan, Nanjing (Nanking), Harbin. | Major ports: Tianjin (Tientsin), Shanghai, Qingdao (Tsingtao), Guangzhou (Canton). |
| Area | 3,695,500 sq.miles (9,571,300 sq. km.) | China is the third-largest country in the world. |
| Terrain | Range of types. Mountains, deserts, and arid basins in the north and northwest. Mountainous in the south. Rolling hills and plains in the east. | Two thirds of China is mountain or desert. The low-lying east is irrigated by the rivers Huang He (Yellow River), Chang Jiang (Yangtze-Kiang), and Xi Jiang (Si Kiang). |
| Climate | Temperatures vary greatly in the arid north, with hot summers and very cold dry winters. The south and east are warmer and more humid, with rainfall all year-round. | |
| Population | 1.26 billion | The world's most populous country. Approx. one in four people live in China. |

| | | |
|---|---|---|
| **Population Density** | Shanghai has 7,000 people per sq. mile; Beijing 1,927 per sq. mile; Tibet, only 5 people per sq. mile. | Most people live in the eastern central region, in the fertile flood plains. |
| **Urban/Rural Divide** | Approx. 382.3 million people live in urban areas, 877.2 million in rural areas. | Despite official restrictions many peasants are leaving impoverished rural areas to look for jobs in the towns. |
| **Ethnic Makeup** | Approx. 93% Han Chinese; the rest are made up of "national minorities." | The non-Han are small in number, but concentrated in the border regions, and thus politically important. |
| **Age Structure** | 0-15 years: 26.4%<br>15-65 years: 67.5%<br>65 years and over: 6.1% (1995 figs.) | |
| **Life Expectancy** | 68 (m); 72 (f) | |
| **Adult Literacy Rate** | 82.2% | |
| **Languages** | Mandarin (official), Cantonese, Wu, and others. There are seven main Chinese languages. All share the same script. Also other minority languages. | |
| **Religion** | Officially atheist. Traditionally Daoist, Confucian, and Buddhist. | Minority religious groups: Muslim, Catholic, and Protestant. |

| Government | Communist republic. Ruled by the Communist Party since 1949. There are other parties, but no general elections on the Western model. | |
|---|---|---|
| Economy | China is moving away from a centrally planned economy to a free market one. State-run enterprises are being replaced by market orientated factories. | Low wages in China mean it is used as the workshop of the world by richer industrialized nations. |
| Currency | *Renminbi*, or "people's money." Also known as *yuan* (dollar). 1 *renminbi* (*yuan*)=10 *jiao*=100 *fen*. There are 1, 5, 10, 50, and 100 *yuan* notes. | In transition from a "soft" to a "hard" currency. Approx 8 RMB to the US$; approx. 12 RMB to the UK£ (2002 rates) |
| Resources | Very many, and more waiting to be exploited. Oil in the South China Sea and in the northwest; vast mineral reserves. Forests in the south. | |
| Agriculture | Self-sufficient in food. China feeds almost a quarter of the world's population from food grown on 15-20% of its land, as the rest is not arable. | |
| Growth Rate | GDP is growing at an estimated rate of 8%, making China the best-performing market in Asia. | |
| Main Exports | Manufactured goods, including textiles, garments, electronics, arms. | |
| Electricity | 220v/50Hz. Standard wall sockets have three connectors. There are voltage adaptors in hotels, but it is advisable to bring your own. | |

| | | |
|---|---|---|
| **Media: Traditional** | State-controlled and subject to censorship, but increasingly independent. *Renmin Ribao* (*People's Daily*) is the official Party newspaper. Chinese Central TV (CCTV) is the state broadcaster, with 8 channels. Also about 300 regional TV and radio stations, and increasing numbers of foreign broadcasters. There are over 2,000 newspapers, 8,000 magazines, and 566 publishing houses. | |
| **Media: English Language** | CCTV broadcasts in English and other foreign languages. There is an active (state-run) English-language press in China. *China Daily* is published six days a week, with a *Business Weekly* on Sunday. In Shanghai, the same company publishes the *Shanghai Star*. There are also magazines that list events, etc. aimed at the foreign community. | |
| **Media: New** | Internet domain: .cn. Internet use is growing. In 2001 there were almost 9 million Internet users. | There are thousands of Chinese-language websites, and every Chinese organization has one or plans to set one up. E-commerce is expected to grow. |
| **Video/TV** | China uses the PAL system. 96% of households have access to TV. | Videos using the American NTSC system will not work. |
| **Telephone** | International country code: 00 86 | |
| **Time Difference** | GMT + 8 hrs | Although China extends across five time zones, Beijing time is used. |

# chapter one

# LAND &
# PEOPLE

## TERRAIN AND CLIMATE

The People's Republic of China is vast. It has a
total landmass of 3.7 million square miles (9.6
million square kilometers), next in size only to
Russia and Canada. At its maximum, it measures
approximately 3,100 miles (5,000 kilometers)
north-south, and 3,230 miles (5,200 kilometers)
east-west. Its land border is 14,168 miles (22,800
kilometers) long. Apart from the mainland, there
are more than 5,400 islands, some just bare rocks
that only appear at low tide.

It encompasses five time zones, east to west.
Despite the great distance, the central Asian
region of Xinjiang is on the same time as
Beijing—which means that in practice it is still
pitch dark at 10 o'clock in the morning. So people
in Xinjiang go to bed at about 2:00 a.m. and get
up around 10:00 a.m!

Most of the rivers flow from west to east into
the Pacific Ocean. The Yangtze River (Chang
Jiang) is the longest at 3,915 miles (6,300
kilometers)—and third longest in the world after

the Nile and the Amazon—followed by the Yellow River (Huang He) at 3,395 miles (5,464 kilometers), the birthplace of Chinese civilization. However, in recent years, the Yellow River has been shortened by several hundred miles for months on end due to drying up near its delta. China's largest freshwater lake is Lake Poyang in the central Jiangxi Province, with an area of 1,384 square miles (3,585 square kilometers), and the largest salt lake is Lake Qinghai in the far west with an area of 1,769 square miles (4,583 square kilometers).

China is a land of geographical and climatic extremes, and temperatures vary widely. Some parts are located in tropical and subtropical zones, while the north is in the frigid zone. In northern China, summers are hot and short, and winters long and cold. In the south, vegetation remains green all year-round. The coastal regions are warm and humid, with four distinct seasons.

The world's highest mountain, Qomolangma Feng, better known in the West as Mount Everest, forms China's western border. It is part of the Himalayan range of mountains, forty of whose peaks rise to over

22,900 feet (7,000 meters). In the northwest is the Tarim Basin, the largest inland basin in the world.

To the east of the Tarim Basin is the low-lying Turpan depression, called the "Oasis of Fire"; this is the hottest place in China, with temperatures of up to 120°F (49°C) in summer. Xinjiang, where Turkic-speaking peoples live, is also home to the Taklamakan Desert, the largest in China. To the north of the capital, Beijing, lie the huge empty grasslands of the Inner Mongolian Plateau. Mongolia is bitterly cold in winter, sometimes minus 40°F (minus 40°C), but it is a very dry and exhilarating cold with many fine, sunny days. Altogether less pleasant are the dust storms suffered by much of northern China when the sand blows in from the Gobi Desert. The south and southwest of China have a much more agreeable climate, with lush green vegetation and beautiful wooded mountains wreathed in mists. The southwest is the home of bamboo forests and that symbol of China, the panda; also of many plants familiar in the West, such as rhododendrons, which were brought over to Europe by nineteenth-century botanists.

Only about 20 percent of the terrain is suitable for agriculture. However, China is rich in natural resources, many of which are still waiting to be exploited. For example, the oasis towns of the vast empty desert areas used to be rich because they were used for two thousand years as stopovers on the Silk Route—from the time of the Romans, caravans of camels would carry silk to the West. Salt from China's largest salt lake, Lop Nur, also went this way. Whoever controlled the oases could tax this traffic, so despite its arid deserts, Xinjiang was an attractive prize. Nowadays its prospects are even more attractive, as large oilfields are being developed by the central government, though not always to the benefit of the locals.

So much of China is almost uninhabitable that, despite its huge size, around 90 percent of the people, mainly Han Chinese, are squeezed into about half of the area. The government is trying to resettle people in more sparsely populated areas, such as Tibet and Xinjiang in the far west, but the Han do not really want to live there (they consider places like Tibet barbaric and backward), and the locals are not keen to have them. The bulk of the Han population has for centuries lived mainly on the fertile floodplains at the lower reaches of the Yellow River and the Yangtze River. These two rivers deposit silt, which makes the flood plain the richest agricultural area in China. This is where the main cities have grown up, along with the key industries.

## CHINA: A BRIEF HISTORY

The floodplains of the east were the cradle of
Chinese civilization. Three thousand years ago,
the Chinese were weaving silk, carving jade,
casting bronze, and producing other alloys;
creating sophisticated pottery, growing wheat,
millet, and rice; and recording events in a written
language of thousands of characters. The
crossbow, used in Europe in the Middle Ages, was
invented in China some fifteen centuries earlier. A
thousand years before the English Industrial
Revolution, China had advanced coke ovens and
steel blast furnaces. Chinese science, transmitted
to Europe in waves, laid the foundation for many
of the constituents of the modern world, while
Chinese art, architecture, language, literature, and
philosophy continue to be studied and admired
by cultured people everywhere.

The Chinese will tell you, with pride, of their
five thousand years of history, but in fact it goes
back even further. Archaeologists have found
evidence of Neolithic sites dating from before
5000 BCE. The earliest-known dynasty was the Xia,
which ruled about 1994–1523 BCE. By the time of
the Shang (or Yin) dynasty, which flourished in
the Yellow River valley in 1523–1027 BCE, a
sophisticated culture had developed, with an
advanced bronze-manufacturing technology, a
written language, and the first Chinese calendar.

## The Mandate of Heaven

The last Shang ruler was a tyrant who was overthrown by the founders of the Zhou (or Chou) dynasty (1027–255 BCE). This period—which saw the introduction of money, iron, written laws, and the ethical philosophy of Confucianism—gave birth to the idea of the "Mandate of Heaven" (*Ti'en Ming*), in which Heaven gives wise rulers a mandate to rule, but takes it away from evil and corrupt ones. The Emperor became known as the "Son of Heaven," a concept that still had potency right up until Mao Zedong's death in 1976. Later, the "Mandate of Heaven" began to incorporate the Daoist belief that Heaven sends natural disasters such as earthquakes and floods to show its disapproval of bad rulers. During the Zhou period the Chinese people's sense of their unique identity and cultural superiority developed. The name *Zhong Guo*, or "Middle Kingdom," was coined to describe the central importance of China: anyone outside it was considered to be a barbarian. *Zhong Guo* is still the name used by the Chinese today.

A time of war and turmoil followed, called the Warring States period (c. 500–221 BCE), in which the Zhou empire broke up into small kingdoms. The moral philosopher Confucius wrote that the Zhou empire had been a golden age, and for centuries afterward, the Chinese would tend to look back to an idealized time in the past.

The Qin (pronounced "Chin") dynasty (255–206 BCE) defeated its rivals and united the warring feudal states into a single empire. They introduced centralized government—with standard weights and measures, writing systems, and money—and built a network of roads that joined the capital (near modern-day Xi'an) to the distant outposts of empire. The Emperor Shi Huangdi used thousands of slaves to build the Great Wall of China (famous as the only man-made structure that can be seen from the Moon), designed to keep out the "Mongol hordes." The grave of the last Qin emperor, Qin Shi Huang, attracts crowds of tourists, who come to see the terracotta army that stands guard over him.

During the Han dynasty (206–220 CE) the empire expanded into central Asia and was further centralized and effectively administered.

The position of the Emperor changed from that of sole and absolute ruler to one in which power was delegated to a highly developed civil service. A complicated examination system, based on the candidates' knowledge of Confucianism, was set up to select people to work as bureaucrats; it lasted more or less unchanged for two thousand years. The Chinese people refer to themselves as the Han, and *hanyu* is one of the names for the Chinese language. Buddhism was introduced from India.

A large-scale rebellion destroyed the Han, and the empire split into three competing kingdoms, resulting in the eventual victory of the Wei over the Chou and Wu. Confucianism was superseded by Buddhism and Daoism; and barbarian (Hun) invasions started in the north. The Sui dynasty (581–618) reunified China, halted the Huns, and refortified the Great Wall.

## A Golden Age

The Sui were soon replaced by the Tang dynasty (618–906). This really was a golden age for the arts and for the country's prosperity. The Tang capital was in what is now Xian; called Chang'an, it was one of the world's greatest cities, rivaling Rome and Constantinople, with a population of one million inside the walls, and a society with many modern features such as commerce, tax collection, civil administration, tolerance of different religions, and a thriving culture. It was especially famous for its poetry and pottery. The Tang continued the building of canals that linked different parts of the empire, and they built inns for traveling officials, merchants, and pilgrims to break their journeys. There were more contacts with foreigners than at any other time until the twentieth century. The Tang provided a model for the later Song, Ming, and Qing dynasties.

The Tang empire disintegrated into the "Five Dynasties and Ten Kingdoms" amid war and economic decline. Nevertheless, this period saw the development of printing.

### Some Chinese "Firsts"

Engraved woodblock printing on paper and silk was invented in the seventh century; the world's oldest surviving printed book is a Chinese Buddhist text printed in 868 CE. Another Chinese first was the invention of moveable type in the eleventh century.

The Song dynasty (960–1279) reunified China and restored order. This was a period of calm and creativity. However the frontiers were neglected, and Mongol incursions began.

Despite the Middle Kingdom's best attempts to seal itself off from the outside world, foreigners continued to find their way in, sometimes as invaders, sometimes as ambassadors or merchants. The most famous traveler of all, the Venetian Marco Polo, visited China in 1275–92. He wrote the first real account of China, of its rich cities, bigger than any to be found in Europe, and of a well-ordered society. By then, undeterred by the Great Wall, the Mongols had poured across the Gobi Desert on their ponies. They made Beijing their capital, and Kublai Khan became the first emperor of the Yuan dynasty (1260–1368). The Yuan were ruthless but efficient rulers; they improved the roads into China and Russia, promoted trade nationally and internationally, and even set up a famine relief system.

Widespread revolts drove out the Mongols, and the first emperor of the native Chinese Ming dynasty (1368–1644) who succeeded them was of poor peasant stock; again, there are echoes of Mao

Zedong in his totalitarian rule, with its stifling of intellectual freedom and personal initiative. Mongolia was captured by the second Ming emperor. The Ming reverted to type, seeing China as superior in every way, with nothing to learn from other cultures. The result was that Europe was growing ever more dynamic and prosperous just as China started to stagnate. Under the Ming, however, there was architectural development and Beijing flourished as the new capital.

### European Intervention

Foreigners not only came overland but also arrived by sea. The first European ships to land in China were from Portugal, then a great trading nation with imperial ambitions. The Portuguese arrived in 1516 and were allowed to set up a trading post in Macau. They were soon followed by the British, the Dutch, and the Spanish. The Ming had been succeeded by another non-Chinese dynasty, the Qing (1644–1912), nomads from Manchuria, who like all the others soon assimilated into Chinese culture.

The Qing government kept the foreigners as far away from them as possible, by making them stay in Canton (Guangzhou). But this did not prevent the start of a trade that was to become a byword for Western arrogance at its worst: the sale by the British of Indian-grown opium to the Chinese.

Although from a modern viewpoint selling opium in return for tea and silk seems no better than drug pushing, in fact opium had been used for centuries for pain relief, as an early form of antidepressant, as a muscle relaxant, and to kill hunger pains among the very poor. People were aware of the risk of addiction to the drug, but its use was in no way illegal.

**The Opium Wars**

Opium addiction increased rapidly in China, and the Emperor tried to ban the trade in 1800. But the British were at last getting plenty of tea, silk, and porcelain in exchange for their noxious product, and the Chinese middlemen were doing well too. The Emperor's decree was ignored. The opium trade continued unchecked until 1839, when the Chinese took unilateral action and seized 20,000 chests of opium. So began the first of the notorious Opium Wars (1839–42), with the British attacking Canton; Britain forced China to cede Hong Kong and open five ports to European trade. There were to be another three of these wars in the nineteenth century, fought with Russian, French, and American support, and poisoning the Chinese view of Western "foreign devils" for the next hundred years.

By 1860 the West had won huge concessions: foreigners could settle in many different parts of China, exempt from Chinese laws, and the Chinese were forced to pay large war indemnities. As the nineteenth century drew to a close, the Throne of Heaven was occupied by a minor, the four-year-old Emperor Kuang Hsu, but real power lay in the hands of his aunt, the Dowager Empress Tzu Hsi, who, rather than move China forward into the industrial age, presided over its total disintegration.

The European imperial powers were attacking on all sides: in 1883 France took Vietnam, and eventually Laos and Cambodia, from China; the British took over Burma; Japan made a bid for Korea and Taiwan; and by 1898, Russia, Britain, France, and Germany were all set to carve up the rest of China between them. Partition was prevented just in time by the USA's proposal for an open-door policy instead of "spheres of influence."

**The Boxer Rebellion**
Worse was to come. The Dowager Empress raised taxes and added to the misery of the peasantry. War, floods, famine, and drought plagued the last years of the dying century, with the foreign powers profiting at China's expense. Peasant anger erupted in the Boxer Rebellion.

The anti-Western Society of the Harmonious Fist, popularly known as the Boxers, was born in

Shangdong province and nurtured by the
weakened Qing government who saw their
popularity with the peasantry as a chance to get
the foreigners out of China and to hang on to
power. The Boxers massacred foreign missionaries
and Chinese Christians, destroyed churches
and railway lines, and then, in 1900,
marched to Beijing and attacked the
foreign compounds. Rapid
intervention by foreign troops
meant that they lost this battle, but
more and more secret societies were
springing up all over China, aimed at
toppling the Qing dynasty and getting rid
of the foreign powers. Dr. Sun Yat Sen, still revered
as the father of modern China, became the leader of
one of these groups, the Guomindang (National
People's Party) in 1905, and events started to move
fast. The Dowager Empress died at last, in 1908, as
did Kuang Hsu, and the two-year-old Pu Yi came to
the throne—later to be immortalized in Bertolucci's
film *The Last Emperor*. The little boy's reign was
very brief. Revolution broke out in 1911. The Qing
government finally acknowledged defeat, and in
1912 Sun Yat Sen proclaimed the Republic of China.

**Warlords, Nationalists, and Communists**
After the abdication of the infant emperor,
General Yuan Shih-Kai became dictator. On his

death in 1916 effective cental government collapsed. Internal feuding, extreme poverty, warlordism in the north, and lawlessness became rife, and Japan had not given up its imperial ambitions. In 1919 it was ceded Germany's Chinese possessions. In 1921 Sun Yat Sen was elected President of the nominal National Government. The same year saw the founding of the Chinese Communist Party, which had strong links with the new Soviet regime in neighboring Russia. From 1923 the Communists worked with the Guomindang to reunite China, and gradually won the support of the Chinese peasants. Sun Yat Sen died in 1925, and the new leader of Guomindang, Chiang Kai Shek, declared war on the Communists, instead of uniting with them.

The civil war that began in 1926 ushered in terrible times: children worked in factories for twelve hours a day, people starved to death on the streets, and every night carts collected hundreds of corpses as though they were so much rubbish. While the Communists and the Guomindang fought each other for control of China, the Japanese overran Manchuria in 1932, setting up the puppet state of Manchukuo, and then in 1937 attacked Shanghai. During the Second World War the various political groups united against the Japanese invaders. From 1941 Chiang Kai Shek received help from the USA and Britain.

In 1934–5 the Communists undertook the "Long March" from southeast to northwest China to escape encirclement by the Guomindang. Open civil war resumed in 1946, and in 1949 the Red Army led by Mao Zedong defeated the Nationalists at Nanjing. Chiang Kai Shek fled to the island of Formosa (now Taiwan), taking with him the entire gold reserves of his impoverished country. On October 1, 1949—now National Day and a public holiday—Mao Zedong declared the People's Republic of China a reality.

### The People's Republic

For a while, daily life improved for most Chinese, and many look back on the 1950s as the best period of Mao's rule. But in 1958 the "Great Leap Forward," the extremist five-year plan to accelerate the economy, marked the beginning of campaigns that were driven by ideology rather than economic pragmatism. As ever, natural disasters on a huge scale also played their part: floods and droughts in 1959 and 1960 ruined two harvests, and led to famine; and, worst of all, after the Sino-Soviet split in 1960 the Soviet Union stopped giving aid to China. Mao fell out of favor, and for a while, in the mid-1960s, Deng Xiao Ping (who would later become president) and Liu Shaoqi held power. Free markets were encouraged, the peasants were allowed to own their land, and the Soviet-influenced policies that had failed so disastrously were abandoned.

**Permanent Revolution**

Mao felt that China was slipping back into its bad old capitalist ways, and retaliated by unleashing the "Great Proletarian Cultural Revolution," whose shock troops were the Red Guards. Its aim was "to hold aloft the banner of Mao Zedong's thought . . . struggle against the capitalist roaders . . . and to transform education, literature, and art . . . to facilitate the development of the socialist system." From 1965 until Mao's death from Parkinson's disease on September 9, 1976, China was engulfed in cruelty and orchestrated chaos. Schools and universities closed, teachers were humiliated and persecuted; anyone labeled an intellectual or a capitalist could be tortured, killed, or sent to labor in atrocious conditions; the only music allowed was one of eight "Revolutionary Model Operas" that Mao's wife, Jiang Qing, considered suitably proletarian; bookshops sold Mao's *Little Red Book* of thoughts and very little else. Millions died, some committing suicide in despair. It is almost impossible to reconcile this period of collective madness and brutality with today's vibrant, confident China—but it happened.

## The Open Door Policy

Mao had, in fact, belatedly supported the efforts of Prime Minister Zhou Enlai to restore order in 1970. A window of opportunity opened in 1972 with President Nixon's visit to China. Eventually, after Mao's death and the arrest of his wife Jiang Qing and the other members of the infamous "Gang of Four," in 1977 Deng Xiao Ping, supreme pragmatist and a survivor against all the odds, returned to power. Deng's greatest achievement was the "Open Door Policy" that put China back into the global community on which it had for so long turned its back. Deng was a pragmatist: his famous statement that "It does not matter what color the cat is, so long as it catches mice" was the antithesis of Mao's dogmatism. He introduced market incentives and encouraged foreign trade, and his pragmatic economic policies have been accelerated by his successors.

Since 1979, China's economy has doubled roughly every seven-and-a-half years. The country is self-sufficient in food. Most children have access to vaccines, clean drinking water, and basic health care. Life expectancy has increased. After a century of trauma, the Chinese people today are rebuilding civil society.

Milestones at the end of the twentieth century were the events in Tiananmen Square in 1989, which, though shocking, did not plunge China back into turmoil as many had feared; and the peaceful handover of the British-leased territory of Hong Kong back to Chinese rule in 1997.

The twenty-first century has already produced three more milestones: China's successful bid to host the Olympics in 2008; its unequivocal support for the US-led antiterrorism campaign; and, probably the most significant of all, its entry into the World Trade Organization in 2001, after fifteen long years of negotiations.

## THE GROWTH OF NEW CITIES

China is the most populous country in the world. For thirty years after the founding of the PRC, couples were encouraged to produce more revolutionaries and the population doubled. "The more Chinese, the better," said Mao; so the traditional Chinese desire for big families went unchecked until 1979. Since then the government has tried by every possible means to enforce the unpopular One Child family policy. It has had much success in the cities among the educated middle classes, less in the countryside where more than two-thirds of the people still live. Even by official Chinese estimates, 25 million babies are born each year, and in common with other rapidly industrializing countries, the Chinese are now living to a ripe old age, adding to the population burden at the other end of the scale.

The recent economic reforms have caused huge regional disparities and growing economic stratification. Approximately 2.8 million households had an annual income of 100,000 RMB in 2001, but the subsistence class, approximately 106.2 million households, had an annual income of 5–10,000 RMB. Despite official restrictions on taking up residence in the towns, peasants are leaving impoverished parts of the countryside to find work in the cities.

The general economic trend is improving, however. In 1978 there were 250 million people living in abject poverty, about 26 percent of the rural population. By 1994, this had been reduced to 80 million, and it is due to be halved again. Most Chinese have become relatively prosperous in the past twenty years, and the World Bank estimates that by 2020 per-capita income will be approaching that of Portugal in the 1990s, still less than half that of the United States.

In order to ease the pressure on the swelling cities, the Chinese government, as well as dispersing the population to other areas of the country, is building brand-new cities. The number of cities with a population of more than

500,000 has increased from twelve to eighty-one. Beijing, Shanghai, and Chongqing are three of the most densely populated, with Shanghai clocking up a tremendous 7,000 people per square mile (2,700 per square kilometer). By way of contrast, Tibet has just five people in the same amount of space. These eastern cities, though crowded, are much wealthier and are much better served by good schools, hospitals, and libraries than are the more remote areas. There are more shops, a much greater variety of goods, more culture, and far more opportunities both for native Chinese and for the foreign businessperson.

## HAN CHINESE AND MINORITY NATIONALITIES

Ninety-two percent of the population of China are of the Han race, or what the West calls Chinese. Minority nationalities generally live in the northwestern and southwestern extremities of the country, and tend to stay there rather than move around and integrate with other ethnic groups. Fifty-five minority nationalities are officially recognized, totalling just over 100 million people. They have their own customs, languages, dress, and religions. Many in the northwest, near the borders with Pakistan, Afghanistan, India, and Russia, follow Islam. Tibetans, Mongolians, Lobas,

Moinbas, Tus, and Yugurs are Lamaists. The Dai, Blang, and Deang people are Buddhists. A considerable number of the Miao, Yao, and Yi people are Christian. Official attitudes toward their different customs are a complex mixture of tolerance and control. They are exempted from the One Child policy, but the ancient Chinese belief in the superiority of Han Chinese culture is as strong as ever in regions like Tibet or Xinjiang.

Mandarin is promoted throughout China as the official spoken language of the country, and all minority peoples are urged to learn it. But the government has also helped to create written languages for ten minority nationalities, including the Zhuang, Bouyei, Miao, Dong, Hani, and Li, which prior to 1949 had only spoken languages.

Although the minority nationalities represent a comparatively small proportion of China's total population, they have a geopolitical importance far beyond their numbers because of the strategic territories they occupy along China's sparsely populated and porous frontiers.

## GOVERNMENT AND POLITICS

Although often seen as a one-party state, China has eight "democratic parties," some of them formed more than fifty years ago, which have an advisory role to the Communist Party. The Communist Party of China was founded on July 1, 1921. Currently, it has more than 58 million members, with over 3.3 million grassroots branches. But membership is no longer a prerequisite for getting a good job.

The State Council, which is the highest level of state administration in China, is the Central People's Government. Under this are a whole swathe of commissions, ministries, provincial governments, and corporations. The State Planning Commission and the State Commission for Restructuring the Economy coordinate policy at the national level. China is still a very slow and bureaucratic society, unused to the rapidity of decision making and the freedoms of North America and Western Europe, and of course the government is not democratically elected. But compared to the period right up to the late 1990s, when the dead hand of state interference blighted any attempt at doing business, or any individual initiative whatsoever, these are halcyon days.

Political stability has increased, attempts have been made to root out official corruption, many unnecessary layers of government have been abolished, and a start has been made on developing the rule of law. This is potentially the biggest change of all, and means that the private citizen is theoretically able to take corrupt officials to court for the first time (though it is still far from easy to do), and also that foreign companies have at least nominal legal protection, thanks to the increasingly sophisticated system of commercial law. Individual Chinese organizations can now have access to foreign currency, and can make their own arrangements to meet foreign partners, produce or market a product, or travel abroad. As with most developing nations that are moving from a centrally planned to a market economy, the closure of inefficient state enterprises has brought unemployment, poverty, and social unrest, but at least new businesses are able to move in to take up the slack.

The price of China's membership of the World Trade Organization, the subject of years of protracted negotiations, was that it had to agree to open scrutiny of legal processes, to cutting import tariffs, to applying international safety and inspection measures, and to putting an end to the piracy of other countries' products, which is rife at present. Some companies in China are worried that the price is too high, but in the long term, entry should help to strengthen the rule of law and the country's stability and prosperity.

## FREE SPEECH AND OTHER ISSUES

The media in China are state controlled, but this simple statement belies the huge growth in the number and type of publications, as well as in independent and pirate radio and TV stations, TV and radio beamed in from other countries, and, of course, increasing access to the Internet as well as to foreign travel.

Most Chinese people are naturally reticent about criticizing their country to a foreign visitor, at least until they know and trust him or her. Hard-hitting interviews with politicians on television are almost unheard of; news broadcasts are usually prerecorded, not live. News bulletins will still take several days (or weeks) to report on domestic disasters such as fires or industrial accidents, while gleefully dwelling on those in other countries (often, ironically, by using film footage from those countries' own uncensored news programs), and they will still concentrate on the heroic efforts of the People's Liberation Army to rescue flood victims rather than investigate whether the flood was caused by official mismanagement or environmental degradation. But, like everything else in China, things are changing fast, and the younger generation has little patience with the old Confucian/Marxist conventions that put officials above criticism.

The Chinese are avid readers. There are 566 publishing houses in China, more than 8,000 periodicals, and 2,053 newspapers. *Renmin Ribao* (*People's Daily*) is the official newspaper of the CPC Central Committee and *Qiushi* (*Seeking*

*Truth*) is its theoretical publication. There is an active English-language press, all State-run. The main publication is *China Daily*, published six days a week, with a *Business Weekly* on Sunday, running from eight to twelve pages. In Shanghai, the same company publishes the *Shanghai Star*. There are a number of magazines, mainly intended for overseas circulation, such as the weekly *Beijing Review* (a political and economic news digest), and the monthly *China Today*, *China Pictorial*, *Women of China*, *China Literature*, and *China's Tibet*.

The question of human rights is a thornier issue, partly because of the different interpretations put on it in the West and in China. The harsh penal system, the government's intolerance of any perceived or direct challenge to the rule of the Communist Party, the frequent use of the death penalty, and the nature of Chinese rule over regions where there are substantial ethnic minorities, are all flashpoints. The often undisputed and misused power of local village officials over poor peasants is another cause of much human misery in the remote rural areas where few foreigners ever venture. Reforms passed in Beijing take time to reach the countryside. However, increasing prosperity, legality, and contact with other societies can only strengthen the drive for civil liberty in China.

## THE ENVIRONMENT

Years of booming population, food shortages, heavy industrialization, and complete disregard for the environment has had a disastrous effect on China's wildlife. Many less-educated Chinese people regard animals solely as a source of food, except for those creatures also unlucky enough to be thought to have medicinal properties (for example tigers, whose ground-up bones are used to enhance male potency). In the outdoor food markets in southern China almost everything is sold while still alive, as this is a guarantee of freshness; seeing many threatened species, such as musk deer, pangolins, raccoons, and tiny monkeys, cooped up in cramped, filthy cages waiting to be killed and cooked can be distressing.

However, there is now hope of reversing the worst of the damage. More than 300 nature reserves have been established, which protect over 1.8 percent of the land area. Many animals are, officially at least, protected. Illegal hunting and trapping continues, of course, but in the battle between conservationists and poachers, at least the conservationists have the law on their side.

What about industrial pollution? Here, too, things are slowly getting better. Since China opened up again in 1979, Chinese and international experts have been cooperating on a wide range of long-term environmental projects across the country, tackling problems ranging from soil erosion and the melting of the permafrost in Gansu province to polluted rivers in Shanghai. Beijing has been thoroughly cleaned up to host the Olympics in the year 2008. Another hopeful sign is that CCTV, China's national broadcast network, is now putting out programs about the environment that are an honest attempt to explore the problems and to re-educate a population who were told for decades of the benefits of heavy industry and relentless urbanization but not of the costs.

## HONG KONG, TAIWAN, AND MACAU

For many years, English-language maps printed in China showed Hong Kong with the letters "oc. GB" after its name, standing for "occupied by Great Britain." Hong Kong, along with Portuguese "occupied" Macau, is now safely back as part of the PRC. Only Taiwan remains as a thorn in the side of the Chinese government, though now that both Chinas have embraced the free-market economy and the United States' support for Taiwan is more muted, things may ease up a little. Despite the rhetoric, there are many business contacts between the PRC and the ROC, or Republic of China, as Taiwan is called.

## Taiwan

Taiwan has its own government and currency, but its sovereign status is ambiguous. The major world powers acknowledge China's claims to Taiwan, and only a handful of countries officially recognize it as a nation state.

The politically dominant "mainlanders" and their descendants comprise 11 percent of the island's population and are still closely associated with Chiang Kai Shek's defeated Nationalists. The majority, the Taiwanese, are descendants of earlier Han Chinese immigrants, and there is a history of resentment of political dominance by the "mainlanders." There are also so-called "aboriginals" who speak languages belonging to the Austronesian family and have close cultural affinities with maritime Southeast Asia. Almost everybody in Taiwan subscribes to a fourfold division of the island's population—"Taiwanese" (*tai wan sheng*), "Mainlanders" (*wai sheng jen*), "Hakka" (*k'o chia jen*), and aborigines (*shan ti jen*)—though this provides at best a rough-and-ready guide to the country's cultural complexities.

## Hong Kong

Hong Kong has retained many of the traditions that were banned for years in the PRC, side by side with the tremendous vibrancy and the work ethic that have made it so successful economically.

There is a relatively free press, too, and many of the fashions, songs, and "lifestyle choices" made by the inhabitants of Hong Kong are very attractive to the rest of China, especially the Cantonese-speaking south—Cantonese is the language of Hong Kong. Until the return of Hong Kong to China in 1997, illegal immigrants were stopped by the British police every day trying to cross over the wire fences of the border, or swim to the island through the shark-infested seas. Ironically enough, this is still going on—except that it is now the Chinese police who have the task of preventing poor Chinese migrants from coming to feast off the Hong Kong honeypot.

**Macau**
Macau was never as wealthy as Hong Kong, and therein lies much of its unspoiled charm. When the British ruled Hong Kong, and the Portuguese Macau, thousands of Hong Kong Chinese would take the ferry over to Macau every weekend to indulge their passion for gambling. Casinos were forbidden by the British, but the gamblers were free to do as they pleased in Macau, which welcomed the trade as it had little other source of income. Gambling, along with many other previously forbidden pleasures, has made a comeback in China, though not in a big way, yet. Macau's casinos are as noisy and busy as ever though.

## THE OVERSEAS CHINESE, AND CHINA'S INFLUENCE ON ITS NEIGHBORS

Historically, Chinese civilization had a strong influence on neighboring countries, notably Vietnam and Korea, and to a lesser extent Japan. The majority of Southeast Asian countries lay outside direct Chinese control, though many paid tribute to the emperor. However, pressure of population in China itself, plus invasions, civil wars, and economic problems, has meant that for centuries there has been a steady flow of people leaving China. The earliest emigrants were traders and craftsmen who moved to Southeast Asia, where they continue to play a dominant role in business throughout the region. These Chinese migrants may be divided into two groups: the "Straits" Chinese, who are the descendants of pre-nineteenth-century migrants; and the nineteenth- and twentieth-century migrants from South China: Cantonese, Teochew, Hakka, and Hokkein.

Later, in the nineteenth century, laborers or "coolies" (from the Chinese words *ku li*, or "bitter strength") were recruited in very large numbers from south China for work in British, French, and Dutch colonies, and in the Americas. By the 1930s, there were nearly ten million overseas Chinese, and many of the descendants of those laborers still live in Chinese communities in their adopted countries today.

Traditionally, overseas Chinese have sent money back home to their families, and the very successful ones have invested in factories back in their homeland or endowed universities. Many workshops and factories in southern China are run by émigré Chinese from Hong Kong and Taiwan, but the working conditions in some of these factories are less than ideal. The attitude of the mainland Chinese to their overseas cousins is often a rather unpleasant mixture of resentment and grudging admiration, and it can be harder for such people to be accepted than for foreigners.

| CHINESE SOUTHEAST ASIAN DIASPORA | |
|---|---|
| Indonesia | 7.2m |
| Thailand | 5.8m |
| Malaysia | 5.2m |
| Myanmar | 1.5m |
| Philippines | 0.8m |
| Singapore | 2.0m |
| Vietnam | 0.8m |
| Rest of Asia & Australia | 1.8m |

(*Overseas Chinese Economy Yearbook*) (m = million)

# chapter two

# VALUES & ATTITUDES

## CHINESE PHILOSOPHY

The history of China has been built on social order (albeit not always combined with social justice), and that remains true to this day. As far as the Han Chinese are concerned, the four major cultural factors that have influenced the development of their society in the past three millennia are Confucianism, Legalism, Daoism, and Maoism/Marxism.

### Confucianism

The ethical system first laid down by Confucius in the sixth century BCE emphasized personal virtue, promotion on merit by scholarship, devotion to the family, and justice. Mao Zedong may have elevated devotion to the "people" or State above the family, but the essentially conservative tenets of the sage are now being invoked by the Communist Party again in the interests of creating a more civilized, united nation. For contemporary Chinese, Confucianism has good and bad points. In representing the Chinese spirit and culture for so long, it is credited with helping the country survive numerous trials and difficulties, and its teachings are seen as compatible with the need for courtesy, justice, honesty, and honor. Others argue that Confucianism was the strongest bulwark of the monarchy and of feudalism, and hence is irrelevant today.

## Legalism

The Legalists, who had their brief moment of glory at the time of the Qin emperor Shi Huangdi's reunification of the divided land in 211 BCE, had a less charitable view of human nature and of the potential for individuals to achieve social order on their own. To the Legalists, man essentially was born sinful, and only the full force of arbitrary law ruthlessly applied could quell his baser impulses.

## Daoism

The joyful, irreverent, quietist philosophy of Daoism, enunciated by the sage Lao Zi (born about 570 BCE), rejected both the moral idealism of Confucianism and the laws of Legalism as products of social contrivance, leading to hypocrisy or to exploitation. For the Daoists, justice flowed from living in a state of harmony with the natural world around us.

### Marxism/Maoism

The writings of Karl Marx, which had such an influence on the nineteenth- and twentieth-century revolutionaries, were rooted in the rationalism of the Enlightenment and the morality of the Judeo-Christian religious tradition. Dr. Sun Yat Sen, as well as many of the early Chinese revolutionaries, was also influenced by Christian ideas of good and evil. Basic concepts of social justice, the equality of all men, looking after the poorest members of society, and sharing wealth fairly were fundamental to his thinking. The early revolutionaries were searching for an ideology to guide them in their struggle to free the peasants and working classes from what they saw as exploitation by the landlords and the factory and mill owners, who were in collusion with the ruling elite.

The Chinese Communist Party borrowed many ideas from its Soviet counterpart, and it was not really until 1949 that Mao Zedong's thought developed independently. Mao constantly urged the Chinese to identify with the peasants and with the poorer members of society, so the slogan "the poorer the better" became part of China's thinking in the 1950s, '60s, and '70s. People shunned personal adornment, such as jewelry, or pictures on their walls, and if someone had a new jacket or pair of trousers, they would hide it under an old, torn one. The metaphor of the "iron rice bowl" is also part of Maoist philosophy. People were allocated a secure (but low-paid) job for life and an iron rice bowl to eat from that could never break, but the bowl was only filled with a small quantity of low-quality rice.

At first the Communists followed their own philosophy—but this self-denial did not last. By the 1960s, sheltered behind high walls, the new Communist emperors were starting to partake of many of the pleasures of life that they did not allow anyone else to enjoy. The official Chinese verdict on Mao nowadays is that he was "70 per cent good, 30 per cent bad" and that the Cultural Revolution was "a mistake." Nevertheless, his portrait still hangs over the gateway to the Forbidden City, and his embalmed body (which may, according to popular rumor, have been replaced by a waxwork) still has a huge tomb all to itself in Tiananmen Square. Children still study some of his teachings in school, and his role in helping to rid China of the Japanese invaders and the Guomindang army of Chiang Kai Shek is undisputed. The slogan "The poorer the better," has long been replaced by Deng Xiao Ping's much more popular version, "To get rich is glorious"; yet it would still be considered discourteous for the visiting foreigner to criticize Mao, even though Chinese will often do so.

Many of these elements are reflected in Chinese attitudes today, especially now that the veneer of Communism seems to be wearing thin. Patience is a virtue inculcated into the Chinese from time immemorial, as they have had to put up with more tyranny, anarchy, and misrule than any Western people. It takes a lot to provoke a Chinese person to physical violence, though the crowded conditions mean that there are a lot of almost ritual shouting matches in the streets.

## YIN AND YANG

For thousands of years, Chinese cosmology has seen the universe as being divided into two opposing yet complementary aspects, the primal forces or modes of creation of *yin* and *yang*. These terms will be well known to anyone familiar with the classic of divination, the *Yi Qing*, or *Book of Changes*. Although they represent polar opposites, as each force reaches its extreme it produces its opposite, creating a never-ending cycle, both on the physical and metaphysical planes. Yin corresponds to earth, moon, female, cold, and dark, whereas Yang corresponds to heaven, sun, male, heat, and brightness. The dragon was the embodiment of Yang, and the sun is still known in everyday speech as the Great Yang (*tai yang*). As Yin and Yang alternate, so night is followed by day, and the seasons rotate. The principles of Yin and Yang provided the foundation for divination, medicine, and cosmological theories. The pictorial representation of these polarities is a circle, containing a dark shape surrounding a bright nucleus, and its opposite. It is a way of showing that pure male and female do not exist: each contains its opposite. This principle of balancing forces is embedded in Chinese thought.

### Feng Shui

The practice of Feng Shui has become very fashionable in the West recently. In China its popularity is waning a little, except in the south and in Hong Kong. *Feng* is the Chinese word for wind; *shui* means water. This refers to the traditional Chinese belief that there are influences in the natural environment that affect people's fortunes. Every hill, field, and body of water is taken into account in matters such as the siting of graves, temples, homes, and, especially these days, offices. Since the calculations and esoteric knowledge needed for choosing an auspicious site are very complex, families or organizations will call in an expert geomancer, often at considerable expense, and consult him before any decisions are made.

Whereas in the West proposals to build new houses or offices on open ground may be objected to on environmental or historical grounds, in southern China villagers often protest against a new building because it would damage the existing Feng Shui of the area.

Pragmatism

A new "-ism" for the twenty-first century! The aim of most Chinese now is to give their children a good education and help them get a decent job, to improve their own level of culture and education, and to be able to relax a little and enjoy life. The young urban Chinese are very like their counterparts anywhere else in the world now—hedonistic, with a lot of disposable income, hardworking, but also fun loving, and not too interested in China's bloodstained past. The peasants, too, have ambitions, and many have become rich. China's new underclass are the unemployed who have no legal right to live in the big cities, as they do not have residence permits, and for whom there is no work back home in the impoverished towns and villages where they do have the right to live. If the system is changed to allow the unemployed to move around the country to find work, it will signal the removal of the last great barrier to individual freedom.

## CITIZENS OF THE MIDDLE KINGDOM

The Chinese consciousness of their own identity is still strong, and they are rightly proud of their ancient culture and their rapid economic progress. But the old arrogance has gone, to be replaced by an excitement about the possibilities of the new world order. There is still a strong undercurrent of nationalism, however, that can turn rapidly against foreigners, bringing echoes of more troubled and hate-filled times.

Many people in the Asia-Pacific region have dwelt on the strange appearance of Europeans. The Chinese described them as ghostlike or hairy. Even ten years ago, the term *yang guize,* "foreign devils," was frequently overheard by visitors to China—although it could equally well be translated as "foreign ghost," which speaks as much of their pale skins and unusual amount of body hair as of their wickedness. In Hong Kong, expatriate Westerners living among the resident Chinese grew so used to being called *gweilos* (the Cantonese version of "foreign devils") that they themselves used the word affectionately to describe their community. As a foreigner in China, it is unlikely that you will ever be taken for a Chinese, and therefore allowances will be made for you. But it is still a good idea to watch what the Chinese people do in certain social and business situations, and to try to behave in a way compatible with this.

Broadly speaking, throughout Southeast Asia, Westerners are regarded as educated and wealthy, though scruffy ones are referred to by the derogatory term "hippies." They are thought to be punctual and honest, if somewhat aloof and unfriendly. Americans and Europeans are, however, not seen as being family oriented, and rumors circulate about the difficulties faced by older people in Western society. Westerners are also often assumed to have lax sexual morals.

Outside the main cities, in the remote rural areas, many people may never have actually seen a "real" foreigner before—though they will probably have spotted a few on TV, as many foreign films (often pirated) are shown nowadays. People of African origin are a particular object of curiosity, and as late as the 1990s African students at Tianjin University told how they had been approached in the streets by Chinese peasants, who rubbed at the skin on their arms and asked them why they did not wash. Other foreigners in remoter areas have found that, even when they try to speak Chinese, they are still not understood because the face that is making the sounds looks so strange!

In the cities nowadays foreigners will largely be ignored, as there are so many of them, but in remoter areas, or traveling on trains or planes, they will be treated with courtesy and as an object of fascination and delight. Most Chinese who meet a foreigner on his or her travels will tend to take a personal responsibility for the foreign guest's safety and happiness while in China.

## ATTITUDES TO OVERSEAS CHINESE

The writer and celebrity Chinese chef Ken Hom has described the strange homesickness for somewhere you have never been as a feeling familiar to the millions who are part of the Chinese diaspora. He writes: "You can go home again. The question is, what, or where is home? To a Chinese-American or any 'overseas Chinese,' emotional ambiguities are built into any answer. The Chinese experience outside of China has created what has been called 'sojourner mentality.' No matter what economic success emigrant Chinese achieve, the pull of the homeland remains powerful."

Yet if you are a visitor of Chinese origin, perhaps one who has grown up in the USA or Europe, expectations of you are likely to be high. You are expected to bring expensive gifts, sometimes for an entire extended family (a village-full is not unusual), and yet be suitably humbled by China's achievements—a slight contradiction. This can lead to problems and to resentment on both sides, as well as genuine incredulity when it emerges that the overseas Chinese person cannot speak Mandarin.

On the other hand, the overseas Chinese visitor can blend into the crowd and pass unnoticed if he or she wants to. The only way a foreigner can do this is by buying a big straw hat to hide under.

## PATIENCE IS A VIRTUE

In the PRC there can be a lot of red tape involved in what might seem the simplest of procedures— buying plane tickets, or changing money at a bank, for example—and it is essential to learn to accept such inconveniences gracefully. Impatience is seen by the Chinese as a serious character flaw. Trying to stick to a tight schedule in China is often not possible, though it is getting easier as more private travel agencies, banks, and other useful places appear on the scene to compete with the slow and sleepy state-run versions.

## LOSING FACE

The Chinese are keen not to be seen to "lose face," or be shown up in a negative light in front of other people. If they cannot or do not want to answer a difficult question, the Chinese may laugh to cover their embarrassment. It could mean that the visitor has said something that has not been understood, or the Chinese person is unsure of his ground on some point. Equally, a foreigner loses face by becoming angry or upset. The phrase "It is not convenient" is often polite code for saying that something is impossible, or difficult, but that the Chinese person would rather not explain all the niceties of the situation at that moment. It is possible to push gently at a seemingly closed door, but do not try to kick it down. You can be a little insistent—but not too much. It is not at all rude to come back to a problem at a later stage, when there has been time for the Chinese person to discuss the issue privately with other people. He or she will take pride in raising the issue again themselves when it has been sorted out.

## MEN AND WOMEN

If you are dealing with someone of the opposite sex, there is unlikely to be any touching after the initial handshake, but members of the same sex do tend to touch each other more than in the West, and women frequently emphasize a point by patting each other on the arm. In some places away from large urban centers, you may well see young people of the same sex walking along the street hand in hand. In Chinese society this is no more than an expression of friendship, just as it used to be in the Catholic countries of southern Europe. There are, of course, gay men and women in China, but the topic is still pretty much taboo and homosexuals have to be discreet. Openly "camp" behavior or dressing outrageously is still likely to draw too much unwelcome attention outside the major cities such as Shanghai or Beijing.

## ATTITUDES TO WOMEN

One of the Communists' painfully slow but ultimately successful campaigns has been to give women in Chinese society equal rank with men. There is still a traditional preference for sons over daughters among the peasantry, which led to the killing of baby girls (an ancient "feudal" practice condemned by the government but which has proved hard to stamp out). As recently as 1949, when the Communists took power, the barbaric tradition of binding women's feet to keep them from growing "big and ugly" was still in force, despite earlier efforts to ban it in 1912.

Another genuine "great leap forward" for women in the PRC has been the availability of contraception and childcare. Mao's statement that "women hold up half the sky" is coming true at last as a whole generation of young, clever, educated women take their place in the world of commerce, science, medicine, and the media. Progress for women seems to be slower in the rarefied atmosphere of Chinese politics. But foreign women traveling in China will not have any more problems than they would back home, and women working there will be accepted on equal terms.


## THE MYTH OF CHINESE INSCRUTABILITY

In accounts of traditional China, Western writers often used to make the point that Chinese people were not given to being direct in conversation, and favored an oblique approach to almost all subjects; in fact you will probably find that the Chinese people you meet, while treating you very courteously, are often much more direct than many Westerners. Once they know you and trust you (which does not take long) they are as ready to show emotions as any other people. You can expect to be asked direct questions about your age, family, marital status, health, housing, car, and salary—and you, in turn, can ask them about the same sorts of things. Remember to be a little cautious (and sensitive) when talking about the number of children someone has. The government's One Child policy has caused an enormous amount of anguish, and is best touched on lightly unless the person you are talking to appears to want to pursue the subject.

Many Westerners who have spent any time in China have made warm and long-lasting friendships with Chinese people. The differences in the cultures are intriguing and worth knowing about, for both sides, but they are not a barrier.

## THE FAMILY

In many rich Western countries, the traditional family (two married parents, two children) is constantly said to be "in crisis." In China it is still regarded as the basis of society and of the individual's guarantee of happiness and security. Rigid rules about premarital sex and living together before marriage are relaxing a little, but unmarried mothers are very rare, divorce rates are low (though rising), and looking after elderly family members at home rather than exiling them to an old people's "home" is almost universal. In southern China especially, the family is often part of a much larger clan, whose duty is to help each other. Frequently, university fees or other large expenses are paid for by distant relations—especially if they live in Taiwan or the USA. Children are expected to show respect to their parents; this is the fundamental concept of *filial piety,* first defined by Confucius. "Filial piety is the basis of all virtue. It begins with one's parents, is kept up by serving one's sovereign, and ends up by establishing oneself [in life]."

Ironically, the One Child policy, limiting families to one child only, has had a disastrous effect on filial piety; it has created a generation of children who are worshiped by their adoring parents, and who, because they have no siblings, have not had to learn the tedious early lessons of sharing and compromising. The Chinese have dubbed these children "little emperors" and they can be seen everywhere in the richer towns, indulging in their favorite sport of "pester power," that is, getting their parents to buy them things. In the rural areas where many families have ignored the One Child policy, family life is less focused on the needs of one small person, more on the need of the whole household to pull together to create wealth (or just to survive).

The Chinese language has a whole range of titles for family members—auntie (*taitai*), small brother (*didi*), big brother (*gege*), and so on.

Although the extended family is shrinking in the towns, these lovely old words will survive because many of them are also used for other people outside the immediate family—rather as in the West, before it was considered polite for children to call adults by their first name, children were told to call family friends "aunt" and "uncle."

## BABIES AND CHILDREN

The Chinese love their own babies and children, and Westerners traveling with their children will find them the center of attention and compliments. It can be a bit overwhelming for very young Western children, unused to so much attention at home, who find their cheeks and legs pinched, and their arms patted and stroked almost beyond endurance, and who may have to pose for endless photos with their hordes of fans (curly blond or red hair especially can attract huge crowds in minutes). The Chinese love of children comes partly from the belief in the need for family and clan continuity, but also it springs from sheer joy in their freshness and enthusiasm in a country where life can still be quite dull, hard, and gray for many.

## RESPECT FOR OLD AGE AND ANCESTORS

Filial piety means that respect is paid to older people, and by extension to the ancestors. Westerners have heard vaguely of "ancestor worship"; a better way to describe it would be respect for one's ancestors. The only down-side of this tradition of venerating old age is that, until recently, anyone who held a position of power was more or less guaranteed to keep the job till he (it was usually a "he") died in office or retired grudgingly at about eighty years old. This did not do much for the country's economy or the chances of promotion of younger people with fresh new ideas. But as the free-market economy takes over, older people are happy enough to retire earlier and enjoy life. Many workers in their fifties have been made redundant and have had to retrain, but at least they do not suffer the same stigma as anyone over forty tends to in the youth-obsessed West.

The traditional festival of Qing Ming, when families bring offerings to the tombs of their ancestors, is still important today (see page 87).

## EDUCATION

The Chinese have always valued learning and respected scholars. One of the worst effects of the Cultural Revolution was that a whole generation lost out on schooling. Nowadays, people are even more passionate about education as they move toward a modern, knowledge-based economy. Chinese school children and university students have enormous amounts of homework, and have to sit for very tough and competitive exams. Teachers and professors are highly respected (though not highly paid). Demand for a good education outstrips supply, and the government has encouraged the growth of fee-paying schools at all levels to help plug the gap. Online education and distance education on the TV and radio are also provided—ideal for such a huge country. Underfunding is a problem, and the government has pledged more money. But parents are increasingly expected to help out and many state schools are now charging fees. In poorer regions, access to secondary (and even primary) schooling is restricted; the World Bank is working with the Chinese government to improve this situation.

## *GUANGXI*, OR NETWORKING CHINESE STYLE

Networking, or using *guangxi*, was for centuries the main way of getting anything done—finding a marriage partner, a school or job for your child, a market for your product, a place to live, or a trip overseas. Favors were given and returned in an unspoken web of complex relationships. The "trusted networks" of the Chinese are based on two or more persons sharing a commonality of identification. On the whole, it is kinship and family ties that form the basis of Chinese *guangxi* because of the moral obligation of relatives to help each other. But nonrelatives and foreigners can be incorporated into the network. Marital, family, and friendship bonds are important in *guangxi*: so are other ties such as exchanges of vows of blood brotherhood. *Guangxi* ties can also be established by appealing to the real or imaginary ties between people bearing the same Chinese surnames. This does not presuppose common ancestry, though early migrants to Southeast Asia often banded together in surname associations to provide mutual assistance.

Friendship ties developed through coresidence, schooling, and other shared social experiences can also form the basis of *guangxi*. The overseas Chinese have long appreciated the value of kinship and locality links in business, in minimizing risks, transaction costs, and the uncertainties of external economic relationships. Their trading networks span Southeast Asia, and can be very helpful to entrepreneurs wishing to set up joint ventures, or to locate new suppliers in mainland China. Many Chinese firms engage non-Chinese partners, but, compared with their traditional bonds, these purely functional ties are less strong.

# THE CHINESE AT HOME

## LIFESTYLES AND HOUSING

In today's more relaxed political climate, it is becoming increasingly common for the Chinese to invite their foreign friends home for dinner, and even to stay in their homes, something that would have been unthinkable a few years ago. The visit can be carried out quite openly. No Party vigilante will be hovering at the entrance to the apartment building inquiring whom you are visiting or why—though curious neighbors may well take this role on for themselves! The Chinese are used to living cheek by jowl, and take a lot of interest in each other's comings and goings. You should be prepared to be the center of attention. Chinese inviting Westerners to their home often invite relatives, neighbors, and friends to drop in to inspect the visitor—especially if some of them speak English or the native tongue of the guest. This is a chance for lighthearted conversation, rather than serious discussion of topical issues.

The Chinese are extremely hospitable. Tea will be served the moment the guest walks through the door, usually accompanied by various snacks, such as rice crackers, roasted watermelon or sunflower seeds, peanuts, or preserved or fresh fruit. One can nibble at one or two of these offerings, but there is no obligation to keep snacking—especially as there is likely to be a substantial meal served at a later stage.

Unlike the Japanese, who generally entertain in public places due to embarrassment at the cramped conditions at home, the Chinese seem to be quite happy to throw open their homes to visitors, no matter how humble the dwelling.

With the rapid demolition of many of the traditional courtyard homes that made cities like Beijing so attractive in the past, most ordinary Chinese now live in high-rise apartment blocks. These tend to be very basic, and even new ones often have a raw, unfinished look. The individual home is likely to be somewhat small and cramped by Western standards. There may be a bed in the living room, which provides valuable additional seating when visitors come. Dinner may be served on a small table crammed into a corner between the front door and the toilet. Nevertheless, from the host's point of view, this is likely to be a considerable improvement on the family's previous accommodation. The PRC has severe housing problems, which it is trying very hard to overcome, so for most people in this overcrowded country the fact of having a roof over their head, a toilet and kitchen that are not shared with other families, and hot and cold running water, is sufficient blessing.

The per capita living space in most major cities is only 76.4 square feet (7.1 square meters). People live on top of each other with little privacy. Conflicts are common over minor issues—a playful child, a noisy radio. A goal of most Chinese is to move into new and larger houses, but prices are high and most will have to wait years for their dream home. But the Chinese can now buy their own homes, and many rich urban couples are doing that; peasant families tend to own their homes anyway, and whenever they have some spare cash, they build another room, or story. (Unlike Westerners, they do not need to worry too much about planning permission!)

As more young people get married, start families, and begin to enjoy more freedom to move around the country (this will increase once the residential permit system is abandoned), the traditional extended family is starting to break up. In the main cities, at least, three or even four generations living under one roof is becoming less common with each passing year.

Although the exterior may not look attractive, the Chinese do their best to make the interior of their own homes as pleasing and comfortable as their limited budgets allow. The homes the Westerner is likely to visit will be fairly well furnished. With growing affluence, the gap between them and the average Western home is narrowing. Invariably, there will be a color TV, a VCR or DVD, CD player, telephone, and, increasingly, a computer. Many Western visitors have realized that their TV and computer back home are more old-fashioned than the ones their Chinese hosts possess. Many high-tech Japanese goods are now manufactured in China, so the Chinese market seems to get its pick of newer models several years before Western Europe does! In the kitchen there will be a refrigerator, a washing machine, and a microwave oven—these, too, are made in China. Manufacturers of dishwashers are optimistic that this will be the next acquisition for urban families. Because of limited space, the home will tend to look rather overcrowded, with every inch of space used for storage. There are rarely carpets on the floors, as the floors are swept clean rather than vacuumed. Many families remove their shoes when inside their homes—take your cue from your hosts.

Entertainment normally takes place at the weekend, especially now that the move to a five-day working week has given urban residents more free time. Both husband and wife normally work, and with the need to do shopping on the way home, the day away from home can be a long one. In addition, even young primary schoolchildren have a lot of homework, and the arrival of a foreign visitor during the working week would not be conducive to study.

Home entertainment centers on the television. Apart from regular TV programs, many Chinese families enjoy watching Video Compact Disc (VCD) or DVD versions of popular foreign movies. These will almost invariably be pirate versions bought on the streets at very low cost— something the government is trying to stamp out, but with limited success so far.

## SOCIAL RELATIONS AND OCCUPATIONS

On the whole, the visitor to China will tend to mix socially with the urban, middle-class Chinese who have a wide knowledge of international affairs and a love of culture. These people often have more in common with the average Westerner than with the poorer, rural inhabitants of their own country. Although the Western visitor may meet other people on his travels, conversation will be rather limited; first, because of this huge gulf in knowledge of the wider world between the poorer peasants and the more educated classes; and second, because of the language barrier— even if you learn enough Chinese to carry on a simple conversation, the regional accents and dialects outside the big cities can be pretty impenetrable even for the Chinese themselves!

The types of jobs done by people in China are not dissimilar from those in the West— teachers, doctors, journalists, businessmen, and so on. There are, mercifully, far fewer Chinese whose lives are blighted by being stuck in a stifling government bureaucracy nowadays, although, compared with many Western countries, there are still a lot of people who earn their living as minor government officials. But at least the trend is for jobs to be awarded on merit and advertised openly in the newspapers, rather than dished out to graduates by the universities, or as a result of good *guangxi*. This means people are not only much busier at work than they used to be, but also have greater job satisfaction and higher salaries. There is greater job security than in the West, and some big state-run "work units," or *danwei*, still provide everything for their employees and their families, from housing to schools to hospital care. This pattern of cradle-to-grave social provision centered on the work unit is fragmenting rapidly though.

## PRESENTS

When Chinese visitors come to the West they invariably bring a number of small, typically Chinese presents for their hosts, and this is a good custom to imitate. For home visits as a friend, or for business trips, small decorative items such as paperweights or Wedgwood china are acceptable. Whiskey (the better brands) and foreign cigarettes go over well, but the Chinese do not have as sweet a tooth as Westerners, so chocolates are out, and so are flowers. Your interpreter would probably appreciate a book or two. For the most senior of the people you will be dealing with, a bigger present would be in order, though if it is at all sizeable it might be a good idea to make it plain that you are giving it to him or her for the whole group. Otherwise, suitable gifts could be company pens (with refills, if needed), or company ties, ashtrays, or small pieces of glass.

It has become harder to find suitable gifts for Chinese people as so many items that we buy in the West, at a mark-up of several hundred percent, are now manufactured in China! But it is the thought that counts, rather than the gift itself.

One custom that can upset the unwary visitor is that if the present is wrapped, many Chinese people will not unwrap it while their visitor is there, but will stow it away hurriedly on top of a cupboard out of sight. This does not mean they are displeased with it; it is simply "not done" to open the gift in front of the donor.

> **Remember This**
> One gift to avoid is a clock or a watch. The Chinese words for "to give a clock" sound exactly the same as the words for "to take someone to their death."

## CHINESE NAMES

In China the surname precedes the personal name, since the family group or clan has traditionally been seen as more important than the individual. Zhang Hua is thus Mr. Zhang, not Mr. Hua. Sometimes, though, the Chinese adopt the Western practice of putting the personal name before their surname. So it is a good idea, especially when confronted with a Chinese name of only two syllables, such as Jing Wang, to check whether the bearer of that name is a Mr./Ms. Jing, or a Mr./Ms. Wang.

In addressing the Chinese people you meet it is best to use Mr., Mrs., Miss, plus their surnames: Chinese people are more formal than many Westerners. The favored all-purpose title used by the Communists, *tongjia* or "Comrade," has dropped out of use in recent years. If you use it now you may find that it makes people laugh. Many older titles have come back into fashion, the Chinese equivalents of Sir/Madam/Miss.

You may also find that the Chinese refer to one another by their job-title—Mayor Wang, Manager Li, Teacher Zhang, and so on. This is a direct translation of the way they would normally refer to one another in Chinese, and is a useful habit to adopt, because you are almost bound to meet several people who share the same surname, and it will help you keep them separate in your mind.

An affectionate nickname for the Chinese peasant is "*lao bai xing*," or "Old Hundred Names." There are in fact four-hundred-and-thirty-eight Chinese surnames, but that is still a small number considering the size of the Chinese population. Only thirty names have two syllables; the rest are of one syllable only, and some of the commonest are Zhang, Wang, Wu, Zhao, and Li. Personal names can be of either one or two syllables and are very often chosen according to a prearranged plan, sometimes one that the family has adhered to for generations. The children of each generation—and this includes those cousins who are children of one's father's brothers—may all have a "generation" character in common: Li Weiguang, for instance, may have a younger brother or cousin called Li Weiguo, and a sister called Li Weiling, where Li is the family's surname and Wei the "generation" character.

The sound and the meanings of names are very important in China. If you can find a kind person to think up a good Chinese name for you, that fits your Western name phonetically and also carries an attractive and positive meaning, then when you hand over your business card, it will have much more impact on the people you meet. When Chinese people choose Western names the choice is equally important, and if you are going to be working with Chinese colleagues and helping them choose English names for themselves, take a name dictionary.

### Names Matter

One English person fell foul of this when training staff to work in a new luxury hotel in Guangzhou. She chose the name George for one young trainee—but when she told him the story of St. George killing the dragon in Roman times (central to English folklore) he was horrified as he had been born in the Year of the Dragon!

It is not considered respectful for children to use their father's personal name, and in more old-fashioned families the wife does not do so either. If a foreign visitor of the opposite sex uses the wife's or husband's personal name this can be quite embarrassing. So if you have a friend called Professor Zhang Dai Lin, call him or her (many names can belong to either a man or a woman in China) Professor Zhang, *not* Dai Lin, or at least not until you know him or her very well indeed.

A more informal way of addressing people is by using their surname and the word *xiao* or *lao* in front of it. *Xiao* means "little" or "young"; *lao* means "old." The cutoff point is around thirty-five; so if you are a foreigner who starts visiting China when you are still *Xiao* Smith, one day you will have to get used to being called *Lao* Smith. Just remember that the Chinese are showing respect for your advancing age, even though you might rather have hoped that no one would notice it. When someone is really old the word *lao* is still used—but its position changes. China's late president Deng Xiao Ping lived well into his nineties and was known respectfully as "Deng Lao." Using *xiao* and *lao* is completely acceptable among friends and colleagues, and foreigners find it a welcome way to handle the intricacies of Chinese names. But *don't* use it the first time you meet; wait until you know someone well, and then you can ask if they mind. As for your own name, in business dealings it is best initially to call yourself Mr.

Smith, Miss Jones, or Mrs. Evans; keep the use of your first name for friends.

### *Separate Identities*

A custom that seems specially designed to fool the foreigner is that most Chinese women do not change their surnames when they marry. It is possible to know Mrs. Hu and Mr. Li for a long time without realizing that they are actually married to each other!

## OVERCOMING THE LANGUAGE BARRIER

Because of upheavals in the education system during the Cultural Revolution and afterward, the amount of English that your Chinese friends and contacts know will vary considerably. English is now taught at all levels of the school system, and the thirst for learning it is growing by the day. But even those who do know some English will have had less practice in speaking it than in reading or writing. Some Chinese speak exceptionally good English; others, of course, may know none at all, having learned Russian or Japanese at school.

Be patient when speaking, use short sentences, speak a little more slowly than usual if you suspect you are not being understood, and try not to use unnecessarily difficult words, or slang. Be prepared to rephrase what you have just said, rather than just repeat it, and be sure not to raise your voice. In Taiwan, many Chinese people are more attuned to American pronunciation than to British. If you are using an interpreter, try not to say too much at a time—give her (or him) a chance to interpret a manageable amount before you move on to the next sentence. It is important to maintain eye-contact with the person you are talking to (though not all the time, of course), rather than solely with the interpreter. If you can learn some simple Chinese phrases (more about this in Chapter 10) you will find it rewarding.

## MEETING AND GREETING

### Shake Hands

On meeting someone, of either sex and any age apart from very young children, the usual practice is to shake hands, often for a much longer time than would be usual in the West. This may be accompanied by a respectful nod. If you are being introduced to a group of people, make sure to shake hands with all of them. From then on, as far as physical contact is concerned, take your cue from the person you are talking to.

**Stand Up**

In the ever-more-informal West, the custom of standing up when someone to whom you have not yet been introduced comes into the room has almost vanished. In China it would be rude not to stand and shake hands with the new person, and to wait until they have asked you to sit down before you collapse back into your armchair. When in doubt in China, err on the side of formality. The only exception is if you are in a formal meeting at a workplace and someone very junior tiptoes in shyly to whisper to a colleague, usually about arrangements for food or transport. Just smile politely; do not leap up and start shaking hands.

**BODY LANGUAGE**

Compared with some of the more deeply religious and therefore elaborately ritualized societies in Asia, such as India, Indonesia, or Japan, China presents little to worry about. Years of identifying with the "worker, peasant, soldier" (that is, the poorest and least educated ranks of society) have made the Chinese relatively informal and relaxed. One thing you are unlikely to see (and which you should certainly not do) is kissing in public; hugging and other exuberant "touchy-feely" Western body language is rare.

Until recently it was *de rigueur* to belch loudly after a meal to show your appreciation: this, too, was part of identifying with the masses in terms of social behavior. The Chinese who have had contact with Westerners have noticed that this does not go over well with their guests, and have abandoned the practice.

Among the poorer people, spitting and very loud throat clearing, caused in the north by the dust from the Gobi Desert, and all over China by far too much smoking, is a widespread and unpleasant habit that you just have to learn to put up with. There have been numerous public health campaigns against it, with limited success. Nevertheless, if *you* have a cold and need to blow your nose, try to go outside the room—it is considered disgusting by many Chinese to do this in front of other people.

You should also make sure that you cover up bare feet in the summer (socks worn with sandals may be uncool in the West but they are a must in China), and dress modestly and conventionally.

## EXITS AND ENTRANCES

Whether you are joining a new friend for a meal, going to an old friend's house, or taking part in a business meeting, punctuality is vital. The

Chinese consider it very rude to be late, even by a few minutes. Of course, if you are unavoidably delayed (traffic jams have become a major problem in China's big cities), you should phone ahead and apologize, as everyone now has access to a phone and often a mobile phone as well.

Chinese people rise early and go to bed early, so lunch will probably be at noon and evening banquets are likely to begin at six. Meals, meetings, and visits will end promptly. Once the meal is over (and it could last for a long time), the visitors may chat for a few minutes but should then get up and go. There is none of the prolonged after-dinner coffee drinking so common in the West, and departure soon after the end of the meal is the rule in China. It is polite for your hosts to come all the way to the main door, or to see you into your taxi, to say good-bye. If you are the host, you should do the same.

## BOY MEETS GIRL

It is only recently that young Chinese men and women have stopped having to ask the permission of their superiors in their *danweis* (work units) to get engaged or married. This was in part an attempt to stop the forced early marriages of old China, and the minimum age for getting married (or even dating) was set at around twenty-five. Things are freer and easier now, though it is still hard for young couples to find somewhere private to go, and almost unheard of to live together before marriage (partly because of the shortage of accommodation). If a Chinese girl and boy start dating, it is usually assumed that they will get married eventually. It is important for visiting Westerners to be aware of this—what they may see as a casual affair is likely to be taken much more seriously by the Chinese partner who may expect and hope that what is for them a "serious" love affair will lead to marriage.

Coupled with the fact that the attraction of life in the West is still very strong, it is easy for foreigners unwittingly to abuse their power. That said, there are plenty of other entertainments available in the nightclubs and bars these days for lonely visitors, men or women.

## HOBBIES

More leisure, freedom, and money have given many Chinese the chance to take up hobbies. These are fairly low-key as the Chinese are very careful with their money, but eating out, playing and watching sports, doing *taijiquan,* stamp collecting, keeping pet birds, reading, playing mah-jong and chess, ballroom dancing and going to discos and karaoke bars, watching TV, going to the cinema and theater, and surfing the Internet are all enjoyed in the cities (there are far fewer facilities in the rural areas). Increasingly, shopping in the growing number of bustling, modern department stores is done for pleasure rather than just to gather the bare necessities of life. The next big boom will be when the Chinese become rich enough for travel abroad to become a reality for the many, rather than just the favored few.

# chapter four

# RELIGION, FESTIVALS, & RITUALS

## MANY RELIGIONS AND NONE

Official policy is to tolerate but not to encourage religion. The Constitution provides for the freedom of religious belief and forbids discrimination against believers and nonbelievers, though theory and practice do not always match. There are many different religions in China: about 100 million people are Buddhists; an estimated 18 million are Muslims; 10 million are Protestants, and 4 million Catholics. These are simply estimates though, as many people in China keep their religion very private.

Although the majority of Chinese are secular and atheist, traditional festivals and the beliefs and rituals attached to them are important in that they give a structure to the year, and help to define the meaning of life and of people's position in the world at large and within their families. One Chinese author writes: "The Chinese are more concerned with propitiating devils than with worshiping gods," and many ceremonies do just that. Legendary

Chinese gods—such as the semidivine Monkey, who accompanied the monk Hsuan-chuong on a pilgrimage, as related in the epic *Journey to the Western Paradise*—seem to Western eyes to be selfish, cruel, and capricious.

## TRADITIONAL FESTIVALS AND NATIONAL HOLIDAYS

There were many festivals in the traditional Chinese lunar calendar, and several of these are still celebrated throughout the Chinese world. The first and most important is known in the West as Chinese New Year and in the PRC as the Spring Festival (so called because in the PRC January 1 is officially New Year ).

### Chinese New Year

This has always been the time for family reunions. It falls around the middle of February, during the slack period of the farming year—in the PRC more than three-quarters of the population work in agriculture—which means that almost everyone can take a few days' holiday.

The atmosphere is very festive—people dress in new clothes, and strings of very noisy firecrackers are set off at all hours of the day and night. The tradition is that this will scare away any evil spirits lurking about, and also welcome in the new year. But recently the use of firecrackers has been restricted in the cities. There is also a lot of feasting.

Families will make, and eat, hundreds of *jiaozi* (stuffed dumplings that are supposed to be shaped like gold ingots and therefore bring good luck), and they will eat much more meat than usual, and perhaps a special sticky New Year cake called *niangao*. Younger members of the family should pay their respects to the older members (and, in more traditional homes, to the ancestors as well), and the children will be given small red envelopes of money. A lot of visiting goes on between relatives and friends, and houses are decorated with special New Year pictures and matching couplets written on red paper. (Red is the lucky color in China.) In many places, this will also be the occasion to watch a Lion Dance, and for all-night gambling sessions. It is also a time for payment of debts.

Each year is named after a particular animal from the Chinese horoscope. There are twelve animals altogether, and a Chinese person will always be able to tell you which animal he "belongs" to—that is, which animal is associated with the year in which he was born. The order in which the twelve-year cycle repeats itself is: Rat, Ox, Tiger, Hare, Dragon, Snake, Horse, Sheep (or Goat), Monkey, Cock, Dog, and Pig. In this system, 1995 was the year of the Pig (as 2007 will be), and 1996 was the year of the Rat (and so will 2008 be), and so on. Just as the different star signs in the Western horoscope, such as Virgo, Pisces, Taurus, and so on, have certain characteristics associated with them, so do the Chinese animals.

**Qing Ming Festival**

On the festival of Qing Ming, which takes place on the third day of the third month in the spring, families visit the tombs of their ancestors, clean them, and make offerings of cooked meats, fish, fruit, and wine. They then picnic on the food themselves, sitting near the tombs. Many families used to have their own ancestral halls where the wooden tablets with names of their male ancestors were kept. (Thousands of these places were smashed to pieces by the Red Guards in the 1960s.) From the tablets, families could be traced back several hundred years or more. In the town of Qufu, where Confucius was born, almost the whole town seems to have the same surname as his— Kong—and can therefore trace their families back to about 500 BCE.

**Dragon Boat Festival**

The Dragon Boat Festival (*Duan Yang Jie*, or *Duan Wu Jie*) falls on the fifth day of the fifth lunar month. It is a very ancient festival whose origins have been lost in the mists of time, but these days it is associated with Qu Yuan, a loyal minister of Chu (an ancient state in the south of China) who committed suicide in the third century BCE by jumping into a local river when the King of Chu refused to listen to his good advice. There are lively races between long, thin "dragon boats" to the rhythm of drums, and these are said by some people to represent attempts to rescue Qu Yuan. Special packets of glutinous rice (*zongzi*) wrapped in leaves are eaten, and again, these are said to have been intended for the fish (or, in some versions, the dragon) in the river, so that they would eat them and leave Qu Yuan alone.

It is easier to see this festival in the south of China, and in Hong Kong, where as has been noted before, people keep more to the old traditions. There is also a distinct lack of suitable rivers available for boat racing in the arid north!

## The Mid-Fall Festival

The Mid-Fall Festival, or the Moon Festival, occurs on the fifteenth day of the eighth lunar month (around mid-September), at a time when the moon is supposed to be brighter and fuller than at any other time of the year. It is also an equivalent of the Western Harvest festival, and celebrates the legend of the moon goddess, Chang-O. Another useful resident of the moon, Yue Lao, a matchmaker, has his work cut out at this time of year, tying couples together with invisible red silk thread.

Like the Spring Festival, this, too, is a festival when the family gets together, sitting around a circular table to symbolize continuity, possibly to sing folk songs (or, these days, karaoke), or to display fancy lanterns, but mostly to admire the moon and eat "moon-cakes." These are round cakes stuffed with a variety of things such as lotus-seed paste, fruit, nuts, ham, or egg yolk. The fillings vary according to the different areas of China. Yet another legend that has become intertwined with the Moon Festival is that Chinese rebels who wanted to overthrow the Mongols during the Yuan dynasty sent messages to each other hidden inside moon cakes. Most foreigners do not find moon cakes sweet enough, but they look very beautiful and make good presents.

| NATIONAL HOLIDAYS (SOLAR CALENDAR) | |
| --- | --- |
| New Year | January 1 |
| Spring Festival (Lunar New Year) | February 11-14 (three days) |
| International Working Women's Day | March 8 |
| Labor Day | May 1 |
| Chinese Youth Day | May 4 |
| International Children's Day | June 1 |
| Army Day | August 1 |
| Teacher's Day | September 10 |
| National Day | October 1 (two days) |

| TRADITIONAL FESTIVALS (LUNAR CALENDAR) | |
| --- | --- |
| *Chun Jie,* Chinese New Year/ Spring Festival | Coincides with the new moon in late January/early February |
| *Yuan Xiao Jie,* Lantern Festival | First full moon after Spring Festival |
| *Qing Ming Jie,* Pure Brightness Day | Third day of the third month in Spring |
| *Duan Wu Jie,* Dragon Boat Festival | Fifth day of fifth lunar month |
| *Zhong Qiu Jie,* Mid-Fall Festival | Fifteenth day of the eighth lunar month |

**Official PRC Festivals**
As well as Labor Day on May 1, there is Chinese
Youth Day on May 4, Army Day on August 1, and

National Day on October 1. There is nothing much of interest for the visitor to see on these days. The traditional Soviet-style parades of tanks and heavy guns along the main streets of Beijing have been quietly dropped; instead people get quite a lot of time off work (something new and much appreciated) and are encouraged to go out and spend money in the shops, apparently with great success judging by the crowds. Avoid going to China on National Day or around the Chinese New Year if you have business to do, as, rather like Christmas in the West, you will have trouble finding anyone in their offices. Christmas Day itself is an ordinary working day in China—but Christmas, Chinese style, has been adopted in the big cities, though with Santa Claus and shopping as its main rationale.

## BIRTHDAYS, WEDDINGS, AND FUNERALS

### Births

The birth of a child, particularly a son, is regarded as a very lucky event; continuity of the family is assured and there will be a feast held a month after the child's birth, in which hard-boiled eggs with the shells dyed red are eaten. There are some traditional Chinese practices concerning the care of the mother and baby after the birth: the mother does not wash her hair for a month as this is thought to weaken her, and the baby is often bound tightly in a white cloth, reminiscent of the infant Jesus being "wrapped in swaddling bands"; this was originally thought to keep the baby's legs straight after birth, though, in fact, if the child's legs did end up bent this would of course have been caused by malnutrition.

Birthdays as such are not usually celebrated in China. By the traditional calendar, age is reckoned from the moment of conception, not birth, so a child is already considered to be one year old on the day it is born. There is a birthday for "everyone," which falls on the seventh day of the Chinese New Year.

## Weddings

Weddings in China have always been colorful and expensive occasions; today at least most modern brides and grooms get to choose their own partners. In the past, it was the family who chose for them, and the bride and groom would only see each other on the day of the wedding.  Traditionally, the one aim of a girl's life was to get married, and men, too, had a duty to perpetuate the family line. Before a marriage, a go-between or matchmaker would be employed to sort out the details of what was basically a financial transaction. When all had been agreed, the bride (who was often no more than fourteen years old) would be conveyed from her parents' home though the streets in a sedan chair to the house of her new husband. No one would see her—the sedan chair was completely sealed, and there are even stories of brides being found dead from suffocation on arrival (which did not stop the "marriage" from taking place).

Another tradition, which the Communists put an end to, was that of the man taking concubines, either to give him more children, or simply because he grew bored with his first wife. In Tibet this custom worked in the opposite direction—polyandry was common (where one wife had several husbands, usually related to each other).

A happy marriage was rare, partly because the husband's mother was often cruel to the new bride. Widows did not remarry, as it was thought immoral to marry more than once. It is not surprising that from ancient times there have been secret societies of women who worshiped the goddess Kwan Yin and vowed never to marry. Many attached themselves for life to rich families as maids, and stayed there safely out of the reach of their parents and the would-be matchmakers.

Marriage in China now is viewed as being for life, fidelity is taken for granted, and divorce is possible but rare. Husbands and wives both work and tend to share all the household tasks and childcare. People feel sorry for someone who is not married, but there is no longer the same social pressure to marry. Weddings in town are celebrated in restaurants amid a great deal of noise, and the traditional color for anything to do with weddings is red.

## Funerals

The many beliefs surrounding death in China have survived into the twenty-first century virtually intact, despite the endless political campaigns of the twentieth. Until recent times it was still the custom to bury clothing and jewels with the body. In Hong Kong, entire shops are devoted to selling paper money, paper furniture, cars, houses, and paper clothes that are burned and placed with the body on burial; even the non-religious will often pay a Buddhist or Daoist priest to say prayers (several hours long) and perform ceremonies for the soul of the dead person. Another custom that would be thought very strange in the West was that of buying the coffin in advance and storing it in the house. The Chinese, in other words, do not need to come to terms with their own mortality; they accept it as one of the most important events in the life cycle.

White is the color worn at funerals. If the deceased has made it to seventy years old—the same age as given in the Bible as the natural life span—there is not thought to be any reason for serious grief, though there will be a lot of noisy ritual lamentation during the funeral procession.

The Chinese believe that the body needs to go into the next world intact, and so cremation is very unpopular. This presents a problem in the overcrowded cities where there simply is not enough space for graveyards. Another problem arising from the strongly held belief in the need for an intact corpse is that organ donation is rare in Chinese communities, though this affects overseas Chinese more; not many PRC hospitals are geared up yet for this sort of medicine.

# chapter five

# HEALTH & WELL-BEING

**STAYING HEALTHY IN CHINA**

If you fall ill in China, you should be able to arrange a visit to the doctor through the staff at your hotel. In the PRC this might entail a trip to the local hospital, but this is only because there is no such person as a general practitioner in China. It is very worrying for the Chinese, who see themselves as your hosts for as long as you are in their country, to have a sick foreigner on their hands, and they will make every effort to see that you are well cared for.

With normal precautions, such as avoiding unboiled water and dubious food sold by street vendors, most of China should not present too many health hazards. In the summer, inoculations against endemic Japanese encephalitis might be a wise precaution. China has one of the highest incidences of hepatitis-B, with about one-third of the world's infections occurring on the mainland. The country is also very conscious of the growth in HIV/AIDS cases since the first one was reported in 1985. Short-term visitors face no restrictions, but any foreigner wishing to work in the country for a Chinese organization has to undergo an HIV test in order to obtain a visa. Foreigners are seen as having a loose code of sexual morality and are often suspected of having sexually transmitted diseases.

Standards of care vary, and you would be well advised to take with you a supply of any medicines and pharmaceutical products you think you may need. Hypodermic needles, for instance, are often used more than once, so take some unused sterile needles with you in case you need to have an injection of some sort.

Chinese doctors will commonly want to give you an injection for even the most minor ailments, but you can always resist and request some other form of treatment. Sometimes prescription drugs that are no longer used in the West turn up in strange places, or are prescribed for illnesses other than those for which they were originally developed. For example, one Western sufferer from asthma was prescribed Valium, commonly used as a tranquilizer. Make sure, before you leave home, that you have adequate insurance coverage, as medical care is not free. Western embassies are a good source of help, and in Beijing, Guangzhou (Canton), and Shanghai there are medical clinics set aside to help foreigners. If you have an accident, try to get a taxi to take you to an ordinary hospital. With the free-for-all commercial climate in China today, there's no knowing what may happen. One foreign visitor who broke his leg called the police to help him and was taken to a military hospital. There they put a cast on his leg and then tried to charge him 10,000 *renminbi* for the privilege— about one hundred times more than an ordinary hospital would have charged.

## CHINESE MEDICINE

Traditional Chinese medicine is based on the understanding that the body is a cosmos in miniature, subject to the same forces of Yin and Yang that govern the phenomenal world, and that our health or illness is a reflection of harmony or disharmony in the flow of *qi* (which can be translated as "vital energy") through the whole organism. There are several Chinese systems of healing, of which acupuncture and herbal medicine are probably the two best known in the West. If you are offered a choice of Western or Chinese medicine, do not automatically feel you must choose the former. Acupuncture in particular (with sterile needles, of course) can be extremely effective for some conditions, as can some of the traditional herbal remedies.

Acupuncture has been practiced for at least two thousand years. According to the theory, one's health depends on having an uninterrupted flow of *qi*—if there is too little *qi*, or too much, or if its flow is obstructed in some way, symptoms will appear that require treatment. The treatment involves the insertion of thin stainless steel needles into energy points of the body where needling is thought to produce the desired effects. The needles are then made to vibrate several hundred times a minute by connecting them to an electric current for a short time. It is especially helpful in relieving deep-seated pain, rheumatism, swellings of the joints, and similar problems. It is also used, with mixed results, to help people to stop smoking.

Instead of needles, some acupuncturists sometimes use mustard seeds fixed with sticking-plaster to particular points in the ear—you press them hard for a few seconds, three times a day, and the effect is said to be as beneficial as using needles. (A good compromise for needle-phobes!)

Some practitioners also perform moxibustion. This is the burning of moxa (mugwort) on the surface of the body for therapeutic reasons. The gently smoldering herbs are put into little glass or plastic cups, which are then stuck on to various parts of the body.

Herbal medicine is popular throughout the Chinese world, and even in the West you may have seen a Chinese medicine shop with its tiers of small drawers filled with the various esoteric and expensive ingredients (animal, vegetable, and mineral) that are called for in traditionally prescribed medicines.

The diagnostic techniques of the traditional Chinese doctor include taking the patient's pulse for several minutes; the speed and strength of the pulse are believed to indicate certain characteristic states of health. The medicine prescribed will usually involve a number of different substances that have to be simmered together for a long time and will invariably taste horrible.

## BELIEFS ABOUT HEALTH

Despite being at ease with the inevitability of their own mortality, the Chinese place great value on various foods, symbols, and rituals that prolong life. There are many symbols of longevity, such as the deer—the God of Longevity is often pictured riding on a deer's back. A perfect, round peach is another symbol, often seen in folk art, as are the tortoise and the crane. The figure of the crane with its wings outspread and its leg lifted up is often used during funeral processions—it is thought to carry the dead person up to heaven. Noodles are often eaten on the day of someone's birthday, because their long strands are supposed to symbolize long life.

Many foods are believed to have medicinal properties: for example, shark's fin soup is thought to protect against cancer, and for almost every illness there is a list of special foods that will be given to the sick person by their family to help them recover. Some of these may seem quite strange to Westerners: for example, headaches are sometimes treated by heating fresh ginger in the fire and sticking thin slices of it onto the forehead. But the remedies seem to work for people who believe in them, and are the subject of serious study in the West. It is remarkable how the Chinese have retained knowledge of their traditional medicine, the Western equivalent of which has been almost totally lost, to be replaced by reliance on manufactured drugs.


## QIGONG AND THE MARTIAL ARTS

Go out into the streets at first light in any city in China, and you will find row upon row of middle-aged and elderly people silently absorbed in their morning exercises, each going through the series of movements that make up the slow, intricate ballet of *qigong*. This ancient form of breath control is both a moving meditation and the spiritual underpinning of Chinese martial arts.

*Qi*, we have seen, is the word to describe the life force; *qigong* is a series of exercises—combining movement, breathing, and visualization—that direct the flow of energy around the body so that it brings physical and psychological benefits to the practitioner. Some take it to the point where they try to perform what are almost circus tricks, such as driving nails through boards. Others practice *qigong* to heal illness by a sort of "laying on of hands." Opinions about its value are almost as divided in China as they are in the West. The most popular aspect of this traditional practice and the related martial arts can be seen in the numerous *gongfu* films, mostly made in Hong Kong and Taiwan, one of which, *Crouching Tiger, Hidden Dragon*, was a surprise hit in the West.

## BATHROOM HYGIENE

Although most Westerners visiting China will use Western-style hotels, where the bathrooms will be similar to those at home, it is quite likely that they will come across Chinese-style toilets when out and about on sightseeing trips, factory visits, or in ordinary Chinese offices or homes.

A Chinese lavatory consists of a porcelain trough set in the floor, over which one has to squat, feet on either side, facing the end where there is a kind of hood. There is usually no lavatory paper (remember to take some with you), and even if there is, the Chinese usually require you to throw it into a special bin after use rather than to flush it down the pan. (This seems to be partly because of the limitations of the sewage system, but also because the Chinese use what is euphemistically referred to as "night-soil" as fertilizer, and they do not want strands of paper spread all over their fields with it.) As a result, public toilets in China, and sometimes even the communal ones in hotels, have a very distinctive and unpleasant smell and are not places in which to linger. It is often not possible to wash one's hands afterward either, so carry a packet of moistened tissues or keep a small bottle of water in your pack. Another treat in store for women visitors is that in poorer places there are often no doors on the toilets, so privacy is non-existent. In remoter rural areas, where foreigners are still a novelty, you can find yourself the focus of an interested audience of local women.

# chapter six

# FOOD & DRINK

## THE IMPORTANCE OF FOOD IN CHINESE CULTURE

Most Westerners will have tasted and enjoyed Chinese food in various forms in their own countries, and may even have learned the delicate art of eating with chopsticks. But they may be less prepared for what the writer Colin Thubron memorably describes as the "passionate relationship" of the Chinese to food. Folk memories of famine are recent (the last were in the 1960s) and there are still areas where people's diet is limited and poor. Refrigeration is more widespread now, but the Chinese almost never eat "ready meals"; food is freshly cooked for each meal, and fish, meat, and poultry are often killed only a short time before they are cooked. Shopping in the markets or shops is done with immense gusto and everything is prodded, shaken, sniffed, and thoroughly checked before being purchased.

It is debatable whether, in purely Western terms, the Chinese eat a "healthy" diet. They eat many vegetables, things are cooked fast so that the goodness is not destroyed, and people eat small quantities fairly frequently—"grazing," rather than eating huge meals at one sitting, which is one reason why they tend to be much slimmer than people in the increasingly obese West. On the other hand they use a large amount of the very salty MSG (monosodium glutamate, or taste powder) in their cooking, as well as sugar; and in some regions of China there is a high incidence of certain types of cancer, due to the overuse of pickling, the only way some vegetables can be preserved through the winter.

At any rate, the Western visitor will experience a fantastic range of different foods, some wonderful (dumplings, tofu, sweet and sour soup, Mongolian hotpot, and hundreds more treats), and some less to Western tastes, such as "hundred year old eggs" or donkey stew. If the Westerner is overwhelmed by a desire for more familiar food, these days help is at hand. In the bigger cities, though more rarely in the rural areas, there are plenty of fast-food outlets selling hamburgers and pizzas; there are some Italian, Indian, Japanese, Korean, and Mexican restaurants, and also newly opened supermarkets (mostly French) that sell the foods of which, in the past, homesick Westerners could only dream—for example, bread, cheese, milk, coffee, and real chocolate.

## DIFFERENT REGIONAL CUISINES

Chinese local dishes are said to have four, eight, and ten culinary schools, depending on which authority is consulted. Canton, Shandong, Sichuan, and Yangzhou make up four of them: if you count Hunan, Fujian, Anhui, and Zhejiang, you have eight culinary schools; add in Beijing and Shanghai, and that makes ten. You should also try the Middle Eastern–type cooking of the Muslim minorities, such as the Hui and Uighur people, whose roadside stalls produce wonderful (and very cheap) lamb kebabs wrapped in naan bread with salad and hot spicy sauce. Here are a few pointers about some of the schools of cookery.

### Cantonese Food

Cantonese cuisine adopts the good points of all other culinary schools, and its selection of ingredients is extensive. River food and seafood are widely used, as well as birds, rats, snakes, and insects. There is a saying that "The Cantonese will eat anything with wings, except a plane, and anything with four legs, except a table." Cantonese cuisine pays attention to the use of fresh ingredients and has unique cooking methods. Representative dishes are "three kinds of snake stewed," cat meat, snake soup, casserole mountain turtle, and crispy skin suckling pig.

## Shandong Food

Shandong cuisine is dominated by seafood, reflecting its nature as a peninsula surrounded by the sea. Typical dishes include stewed sea cucumber with scallion, stewed snakehead eggs, sea slugs with crab ovum, Dezhou grilled chicken, and walnut kernel in cream soup.

## Sichuan Food

Sichuan cuisine is renowned for its searingly hot, peppery flavor. The variety of tastes is summed up in the phrase "a hundred dishes with a hundred flavors." Famous dishes include shredded pork with fish flavor, stewed beancurd with minced pork in pepper sauce, and dry-roast rock carp.

Those who are not used to extremely hot food should proceed with care. The Sichuanese use a special black pepper that leaves the lips numb—a bit frightening the first time it happens, but not unpleasant when one grows accustomed to it.

### Huaiyang Food

Huaiyang cuisine integrates the cream of dishes in Yangzhou, Zhenjiang, Huaian, and other places south of the Yangtze River, stressing freshness and tenderness, careful preparation, cutting skill, bright color, beautiful arrangements, and light flavoring. Famous dishes include beggar's chicken, fried mandarin fish with sweet and sour sauce, sliced chicken with egg white, salted duck, steamed crab meat, and minced pork balls cooked in a casserole.

### Vegetable Dishes

Vegetable dishes have been popular since the Song dynasty (960–1279) and they were greatly developed in the Ming and Qing dynasties (1368–1911). They were divided into three schools: Monastery Vegetable Dishes, Court Vegetable Dishes, and Folk Vegetable Dishes.

The main features of vegetable dishes are their unique style and their health benefits. Main materials include green leaf vegetables, fruit,

 edible mushrooms, and bean-curd products with vegetable oil as a condiment, all of which are delicious in taste, rich in nutrition, easy to digest, and believed to be helpful in preventing cancer.

## JASMINE TEA AND HOT RICE WINE

The Chinese drink large quantities of tea (mostly "green tea," as opposed to the "black" tea that is more commonly drunk in the West) and they add no milk or sugar. Tea is drunk constantly at meetings and at work, less so in restaurants and at formal meals, though it is always available if asked for. It is usually served in mugs with lids to keep it warm. Teabags and tea strainers are not used, and drinking tea without swallowing a mouthful of tea leaves requires concentration: try using the lid as a strainer when sipping.

Tea is divided into green, black, perfumed, white, and Wulong tea. The most valuable green teas are Longjing and Biluochun; black tea, Qihong and Yunfeng; scented tea, Jasmine; white tea, Yinzhenbaihao, Gongmei, and Shoumei; Wulong tea, Dahongpao and Tieguanyin. The Chinese will frequently give beautifully decorated tea caddies of special teas as a present.

Other drinks you may be offered are yellow rice wine, served hot in little porcelain cups. It tastes rather like sherry. More lethal is *maotai*, the Chinese answer to vodka; there are also many light Chinese beers, as well as a growing range of Chinese wines—Great Wall wine is perhaps the best known and has improved considerably since the producers set up a joint venture with a French wine grower. Soft drinks such as mineral water and Coca Cola are available everywhere, and fruit juices made from the exotic tropical fruits grown in the south of China are delicious.

## TEAHOUSE TRANQUILLITY

One interesting development in the late 1990s has been the reemergence of teahouses, traditionally the haunts of the intellectuals and literati, who would idle away hours in stimulating conversation or in composing poems. In workaholic, postliberation China, such establishments were considered a decadent remnant of the feudal society. But with the emergence of the five-day working week, and with more emphasis on quality leisure time, the traditional teahouse is once again blossoming in major cities. Teahouses have one thing in common: tranquillity—a precious commodity in China. The quiet atmosphere is broken only by leisurely music played on the *zheng,* a twenty-one- or twenty-five-stringed plucked instrument, in some ways similar to the zither. Conversation tends to be carried out in hushed tones. Teahouses are located at quiet places in beautiful surroundings, often near lakes: most cities have several now. The teahouse has its own slot on TV too—the British television company Granada has coproduced with Chinese TV a 230-part TV soap called *Joy Luck Street*, based around the comings and goings in a teahouse; it was inspired by the long-running British TV soap *Coronation Street*, whose central location is a good old English pub.

## SMOKERS' PARADISE

Cigarette smoking is widespread among men in China, much less so among women, and at formal meals cigarettes are almost always offered along with the tea. Most Chinese people do not seem to be at all worried about the links between smoking and health problems. It is very hard to escape from other people's cigarettes in restaurants. Young Chinese men set on having a good night out can even be seen holding a lit cigarette in one hand and a pair of chopsticks in the other— managing to smoke and eat at the same time.

# chapter seven

# TIME OUT

## GETTING AROUND

### Two Feet
Going for a walk in the towns is a pleasure. Streets in China are packed, and there is plenty to look at—and plenty of people looking at you, with your round eyes, funny hair, large nose, and differently shaped body. The attention is not hostile though and a friendly smile will be reciprocated with delight. As for walking in the countryside, this is best done down in the south-west, where there are mountains and bamboo forests to wander through; paths are marked and there are old Buddhist monasteries and ancient little wayside inns to stay in.

### Two Wheels
In towns, and in flatter parts of the countryside, many foreigners hire bicycles to get around, and this is highly recommended. Bikes need a good sturdy padlock as they are frequently targets for thieves (even though they have individual registration

numbers just like cars). There are plenty of places to park your bike, where, for a small fee, a vigilant parking attendant will watch over it. When you take charge of the bike, make sure that it works—dud brakes and loose pedals that fall off as you ride along are fairly common.

### Disabled Access

Access for disabled visitors is not good, but attitudes are improving. Deng Puo Fang, one of the sons of Deng Xiao Ping, was confined to a wheelchair after Red Guards broke his back by pushing him out of a window during the bitter power struggles of the Cultural Revolution. He devoted the rest of his life to campaigning for better recognition and more help in China for people with a wide range of disabilities.

### *Flexible Rules*

Individual Chinese can bend the rules and be very kind to visitors with disabilities. For instance, one blind American visitor to the Forbidden City was given a personal tour of the priceless antiquities there by the guide, who removed the ropes separating the exhibits from the crowds, took the man's hand and guided it over everything while describing it to him in detail.

Buses are impossible for wheelchairs, and trains also; disabled toilet facilities are almost unknown. As many deliveries to shops and offices are still made by carts and bicycles there are at least ramps up into many of the shops and other buildings. There are websites that give more information.

### Taxis

The taxi service in most Chinese cities is excellent (another welcome change from the old days) and taxis are strictly metered and controlled. However, most taxi drivers speak no English, so it is advisable to ask someone in your hotel to write down your destination in Chinese so that you can show it to the driver. You may occasionally find that a taxi driver refuses to take you in his cab. If this happens, it makes no sense to argue. One just has to be philosophical about it, as about many things in China that differ from home.

Once you get into the cab, make sure that the driver starts the meter running, and remember to fasten your seat belt. Be warned! Driving can be erratic and nerve-racking,  especially if you are sitting in the front seat! Traffic accidents are very common.

### *Tipping Is No Longer Taboo*

Tipping used to be expressly forbidden in the PRC, and would be rejected if offered. The habit is now beginning to creep in, but should be resisted, or kept to reward exceptionally good service. Chinese taxi drivers will accept a tip if offered but will not expect one. If you are allocated a driver by the organization looking after you, he will be pleased if you offer him cigarettes. The person in charge of you will also make sure that he gets his meals and breaks and so on, so you do not have to worry about his welfare.

## Air Travel

China is a vast country and the quickest way to cover long distances is by air. The Chinese used to have a rather poor record on air safety for domestic flights, but this has now improved. However, be prepared for long delays with no explanations offered. Flying is relatively expensive and not as interesting as traveling by train.

## Rail Travel

This is the way most Chinese people get around the country, but be warned that getting tickets can be extremely difficult and needs to be done well in advance of your trip. Your ticket is good for one train only, so do not miss it! Travel by train is not fast (not even the "express" trains), but it gives the traveler a much better idea of what China is like.

The rail network is huge and seems to be permanently overcrowded, especially at festival times when the whole of China is on the move, trying to get home to their families. You can travel "soft" class or "hard" class, but you may be expected, as a foreigner, to pay more than a Chinese person would.

Soft-class accommodation is very comfortable, with four berths in the sleeping compartments and air-conditioning. Hard-class sleepers are arranged in serried ranks in a sort of dormitory car, with no doors to separate the different sections: they are fairly comfortable, if totally lacking in privacy. Least comfortable, and certainly not to be recommended for journeys of more than a few hours, is hard-seat accommodation. This is usually dangerously overcrowded by Western standards, and although providing an unparalleled insight into Chinese life is not for the fainthearted.

There is usually no separate accommodation for nonsmokers, and Chinese men smoke incessantly to pass the time on long train journeys—sometimes they even smoke in the couchettes, in the middle of the night when everyone is trying to get some sleep! Another problem for anyone hoping to sleep on these journeys is that everyone snores, and if lying awake at home next to one snoring person has bothered you, just try a whole carriage full. The thin blankets that are handed out to the occupants of the hard-class couchettes are rather scratchy and can harbor  some interesting specimens of insect life; bring your own.

## Bus Travel

It is possible to travel by long-distance bus in China, but again this is not very comfortable, especially if you are likely to have a lot of baggage crammed around your knees.

## Travel by Boat

Though crowded, this is also quite common and can be very enjoyable—there are regular boats along the Yangtze River, along the Grand Canal, and up the Pearl River from Canton (Guangzhou) to Wuzhou. (For more information on all these "journeys of a lifetime," the *Lonely Planet* guide to China is excellent, and there are more suggestions for other useful books at the end of this one.)

## RULES AND REGULATIONS

Individual travelers wishing to make their own way can obtain a thirty-day tourist visa at any Chinese consulate or other organization overseas authorized by the Ministry of Foreign Affairs. For a party of more than four people a group visa can be obtained. Visitors wanting to stay beyond thirty days can usually gain an extension (up to sixty days) by applying to the local entry and departure administrative departments of the Public Security Bureau. The extension must be obtained prior to the expiry of the existing visa, and there is usually no problem with this. Business travelers normally require an invitation letter from a recognized Chinese organization or enterprise in order to obtain a visa. Some business people circumvent this by entering on a tourist visa, but this can lead to problems.

Tourists visiting the PRC may wish to leave all the arrangements in the hands of the China Travel Service, which has offices in many countries. In that case, the CTS will arrange all the necessary visas, but the downside is likely to be a highly regimented program with little chance for improvisation.

### Tibet

Tibet is now much more open to foreign visitors than in the past. But tourists need to obtain separate visas, after obtaining permission from the Tibet Tourism Administration or one of its overseas offices. Visitors should try to go there overland—if you fly in, you risk the fate of the Western journalist who spent three days of his four-day visa in bed recovering from altitude sickness. The body needs time to acclimatize to the thinner air of Lhasa, even though it is only 2,289 feet (3,683 meters) above sea level.

## "Sensitive Zones"

Holders of tourist visas must pass through Chinese ports designated as open to visitors from abroad. Although most of China is now open to foreigners there are still some places, particularly in sensitive border areas, that are restricted, and it is advisable to check this in advance. Travelers have been arrested and interrogated for entering these zones, and even expelled from the country.

Foreigners visiting China on normal travel permits may not engage in activities that do not conform with their permitted status, such as taking up employment, study, or reporting. The authorities are particularly sensitive about journalists who sometimes masquerade as tourists in order to gain unsupervised access to strategic areas such as Tibet.

**Taking Photos**

Visits to temples, palaces, museums, and so on are straightforward and demand no special behavior. But remember that it is polite to ask permission before you take a photograph of a person (even though this may result in a request for a small payment). Photographers are not always welcome. In temples, be especially sensitive—there may be people worshiping—and try not to cause too much of a stir by your presence. Do not point your camera at policemen or at soldiers guarding government buildings, and be careful about taking pictures at airports. Railway stations are fine though, and if you like steam trains, China is the place to take your camera.

**MONEY AND SAFETY**

Gone are the days when foreigners had to pay for everything in FEC (Foreign Exchange Certificates, popularly known among Westerners as "funny money"). Nowadays, all cash transactions are in *Renminbi* ("people's currency"), also known as the *Yuan* (dollar), which is what you will be given when you change your money at the airport or at banks or hotels. (It is not possible to buy *Renminbi* outside China, yet.) There are 1, 5, 10, 50, and 100 *Yuan* notes. The *Renminbi* is broken up into 100 *Fen*, and there are coins of 1, 2, 5, and 10. To complicate things, the Chinese always refer to the 10 *Fen* coin as either a *Jiao* or a *Mao*.

US dollars are much in demand, but remember that the illegal money-changers who accost you in the street, and who seem to be active all over China, could get you into serious trouble. Counterfeiting is a problem, and the likelihood of being given false 50 or 100 *Yuan* notes is very high. Exchange rates seem to be much the same wherever you change money, so do not waste time shopping around. There are branches of many Western banks in Beijing now, but you should not have difficulty in changing travelers' checks or currency in branches of the Bank of China, or in your hotel. Keep the receipts of all your money-changing transactions to ensure that you have no problems changing the local currency back into your own when you leave the country, although this, too, is much less rigid than it was.

Credit cards, although increasingly widespread in use, are not yet as commonly acceptable in China as in the West, so you may want to carry more cash on you than you normally would. Watch out for pickpockets, however—also an increasingly widespread phenomenon. There are large numbers of unemployed people coming to the big cities, desperate for work; foreigners are known to be rich. Crime in China is still remarkably low, and many foreign visitors say they feel safer there than they would in the streets of New York or London: muggings and street crime are rare. But be sensible.

## SHOPPING

Shopping is another leisure activity in which the Chinese themselves are now able to indulge. With the advent of joint-venture shopping centers and a much freer market for consumer goods, the wind of competition has swept through China, and there is a much wider variety of goods available at a far larger number of outlets than used to be the case—so much so, that China is rapidly becoming a shopper's paradise. In the main cities, stores are usually open from 9:00 a.m. to 9:00 p.m. seven days a week, and in Shanghai until 10:00 p.m.

In theory, prices are fixed in the shops, but in practice there is often room for a bit of haggling. In the markets it is normal for the price quoted to start at about three times the eventual price you can expect to pay. Many of the new breed of street traders are very astute young saleswomen (men seem to fade into the background in the markets), and will be insistent but not aggressive; they often know not only English but bits of Russian, French, and German. In ten years China has gone from a country with almost nothing to buy (barring the inevitable badly designed silks and rather old-fashioned *cloisonné* enamel products) to a place that manufactures most of the clothes sold in Western shops, including designer-label stores; its factories also turn out hats, underwear, jewelry, handbags, backpacks, furniture, lighting, digital cameras, computers, mobile phones, and televisions for the world market. Never mind bringing an extra bag home from China to carry all the shopping you have done there; soon you will have to hire a small truck!

**What To Buy**
Apart from clothes and other products made in China for export to the West and Japan, China is rich in its own arts and crafts, reflecting its long cultural traditions, and these are flourishing. Carving, embroidery, pottery and porcelain, glassware, weaving, printing, wood carving and dyeing, and perfect replicas of ancient cultural relics are all exquisitely made by hand—labor is still cheap enough for this to be possible.

China's handmade carpets sell briskly on international markets. Some of the folk art is very attractive, too—patchwork for example, as well as folk scissor-cuts created by women farmers—and are all well worth seeking as gifts to take home.

The visitor should be careful about buying antiques. These should be bought at official stores, and will bear a special seal authorizing their export. China has lost enough antiquities one way and another in the past, and is now hanging on to what it has left. There is a bigger supply of legitimately available antiques in Hong Kong, where many were taken by families fleeing the turmoil of the 1930s and '40s. There are, of course, very attractive fakes to be found as well!

## NIGHTLIFE

Big cities in China used to settle down wearily for the night at 8:00 p.m. Now they never sleep. There is an ever-increasing variety of entertainment and leisure activities available in China. Apart from cinemas, theaters, and food outlets (pizzas and burgers are all the rage), there are karaoke clubs, cyber cafes, MTV lounges, bars, and nightclubs, all ready to welcome you and help you spend some money. There are often a number of "hostesses" in these places, both Chinese and Western (especially young women from Russia).

They tend to be heavily made-up and provocatively dressed—the puritanism of the past is long gone. Another taboo that has vanished as though it never existed is that of foreigners and Chinese being forced to sit in different parts of restaurants, stay in different hotels, shop in different shops, pay different prices, and so on. This absurdity was probably imported from the old Soviet Union, which enforced it rigidly—but now the Soviet Union is gone, and so has this unwelcome form of apartheid in China.

## CULTURE

### Peking Opera

A uniquely Chinese form of entertainment is the Peking Opera. ("Peking" was the way foreigners used to pronounce what is now universally called "Beijing," or "northern capital city.") Peking Opera is a form of traditional Chinese drama that has been popular for about a hundred and fifty years, and involves acrobatics, fencing, and boxing, as well as music and singing. The music may sound very harsh and discordant to the Western ear, but the whole thing is definitely a spectacle worth seeing. The actors wear elaborate costumes and colorful, stylized makeup. The audience is almost as interesting as the characters on stage. They will virtually all know the story of the opera by heart, and probably the music too: this means they feel free to get up and walk about during the performance, chat loudly to their friends, buy and eat snacks, and generally behave in a way quite different from the hushed stillness of opera audiences in the West.

### Cinema

Chinese and foreign films are offered and ticket prices are cheap. Young(-ish) Chinese film directors such as Chen Kai Ge and Zhang Yimou have won prizes and praise at foreign film festivals in recent years, with films such as *Yellow Earth* and *Raise the Red Lantern*, but in their home country, their brand of slow-moving "art house" films, beautifully shot in the Chinese countryside, and with a subtly critical social message, are much less popular than they are abroad.

## Other Entertainments

The bigger cities not only offer ballet, theater, classical music concerts (again, with very cheap tickets compared to similar events in the West), but also art exhibitions and various sporting events. These days, there are even English-language magazines that list current and forthcoming events. Outside the big cities, of course, things are a bit more limited.

Banquets are a regular feature of life for the business person visiting China, and for anybody whom the Chinese wish to welcome: visiting students, diplomats, filmmakers, academics, or overseas Chinese coming back to the ancestral home. Return hospitality may be expected, or it may be more appropriate to wait to invite the Chinese in your own country if they plan to visit you there.

# chapter eight

# BANQUETS &
# ENTERTAINING

## THE GOOD GUEST

A banquet is one of the very few occasions in
China where having an idea in advance of the
required behavior really does make a difference: it
feels as though everyone has a scripted part and it
helps to know yours too! Evening engagements
can be formal, so take evening wear. Behavior will
be formal as well. One major difference with a
Western-style meal or dinner party is that
conversation will often be just between the most
senior member of the Chinese organization and
his (sometimes her) counterpart on the Western
side. Everyone else, more junior in rank, will tend
to eat in silence, despite the Western visitor's well-
meaning attempts to get them to join in. This is
worst at banquets with senior politicians, where
sometimes the minister will do all the talking
while his retinue limit themselves to showing
their appreciation of the conversation (or the
monologue). It can be a strain for the Westerner
who ends up having to make all the conversation
in return. It is quite in order for everyone on the

Western side to try to make conversation with their Chinese hosts, but do not be surprised if people are too shy to chat back to you.

## GREETINGS
Shake hands with everyone. Exchange business cards with people you may not have met yet. If you have brought gifts, leave the giving of them to the end of the meal. Tea and snacks may be offered before everyone sits at the table, or you may go to the table straight away.

## SEATING AND TABLE ARRANGEMENTS
The Chinese host, who usually sits facing the door, will place the most eminent guest in the seat of honor to his right, and the deputy Chinese host will place the next most senior guest on his right, at the opposite side of the table. If there is an interpreter, he/she will probably be seated to the right of the most important guest. Age and seniority are respected in the seating arrangements. Hosts and guests will normally be seated alternately around the table.

When you sit down, you are unlikely to find a knife and fork laid for you, so be prepared to try eating with chopsticks. Most foreigners manage to use chopsticks to convey the food to their mouths; very few ever master the knack of holding them properly, which Chinese children learn at their mother's knee. Asking for a demonstration from your hosts can be a good ice-breaker.

## EATING

Banquets can consist of up to a dozen courses, so pace yourself. In the north of China, soup is often served at the end of the meal, which will usually begin with a dish of cold hors d'oeuvres, but in the south of China soup may be served as the first course. The Chinese do not, as a rule, eat dessert, although fresh fruit may be provided—usually oranges cut into pieces. If there is any rice, it will not be served until near the end of the meal: it is seen as a "filler," in case the guests are still hungry, and therefore it is polite to leave some of it in your bowl, to show that you have been well fed and have no need of anything more.

Watch what the Chinese diners do when they help themselves to the communal dish of food—they may use a serving spoon, but it is very common to use one's own chopsticks.

There may also be some "public chopsticks" (*gong kuaize*) that are used by everyone to serve themselves.

Do not be surprised if your host is continually placing the tastiest morsels on your plate—this is one way of honoring a guest, who should always wait to be urged to eat before helping himself. You may be given a hot, damp towel to wipe your hands with. If it is given to you before the meal, you can use it as a napkin for the rest of the meal. If you find something in your mouth that you want to remove, use your chopsticks or the porcelain soupspoon, not your fingers. The Chinese themselves would spit it out, onto a little plate, so that, too, would be acceptable. Lifting your bowl (of soup, rice, etc.) so that it is closer to your mouth is not rude, and makes eating soup and rice much less hazardous.

## Alcohol and Tea

Alcohol is very important for drinking toasts at banquets and formal meals, but the Chinese are not heavy drinkers and tend not to drink without food. You will probably find three glasses beside your plate, one for the very good lager-type beer that is commonly drunk and is not very strong, one for some kind of wine (either of the Vermouth-type, or one of the rather sweet grape wines produced locally), and a small one for a more fiery liquor, such as *maotai*, which is distilled from sorghum and is 65–70 percent proof. The *maotai* is usually used for toasts, and you will often see the Chinese finish off a whole glass each time (but they are very small glasses).

## MAKING SPEECHES AND PROPOSING TOASTS

Speeches, which always end with one side toasting the other, usually happen quite soon after the beginning of the meal. The host will probably speak between the arrival of the first and second dishes, and the chief guest should reply a few minutes later, after the start of the second dish. Take a lead from your host and keep your speech short and fairly bland. Make a few general appreciative comments about your visit, some remarks about hopes for future cooperation, friendly ties between your organizations, and so on—and, above all, avoid elaborate jokes as they are often untranslatable, or at least no longer funny once they have been translated.

### Don't Joke!

A Canadian journalist writes of how he had once been present at a grand banquet in the Great Hall of the People in Beijing. During the speeches, a visiting diplomat embarked upon a long and complicated joke in English. The poor Chinese interpreter, having tried in vain to translate it, finally despaired. He simply said, in Chinese, "The honored foreign visitor has just told a joke—please laugh!"

### Cheers!

At the end of the toast, the proposer says "Cheers!" The Chinese equivalent of "Cheers" is "*ganbei*" (literally, "dry glasses"), but caution is advisable here because there will often be a number of toasts to follow. However, the consumption of large amounts of alcohol at banquets and other celebratory events is being officially discouraged.

If you do not want to drink alcohol, soft drinks (Coca Cola or fizzy orange squash), green tea, and mineral water will be available.

## MAKING POLITE CONVERSATION

If you find that the atmosphere at the banquet is
not too formal, make the effort to talk to your
Chinese hosts, rather than spend the entire time
chatting to your Western colleagues. Talking to
your hosts may seem difficult to begin with, but
is very rewarding. Food is one good topic of
conversation, and the discussion of the relative
merits of different places in China is another.
Don't talk about religion, bureaucracy, politics,
Tibet, Taiwan, or sex. Lightweight topics such as
holidays, tourism, travel, and plans for the future
are fine, and you can talk about families too.

## THE RETURN MATCH

If you decide to arrange a return banquet for
your Chinese hosts before you leave, ask your
interpreter, or whoever is organizing your visit,
to help you. A table plan should be drawn up,
and at the banquet there should be place cards. A
supply of foreign cigarettes is always welcome on
such occasions. Remember that as host it will be
your job to keep plying your guests with food,
and other people in your organization can do
likewise, especially each time a new dish arrives.
Your guests will be loath to help themselves and
will often decline something offered to them
several times before they feel able to accept,

so you will have to keep pressing them to eat. It is hard work being a host and a guest at a Chinese banquet, but they are rewarding occasions nonetheless.

### A Change of Style

Perhaps the very formal banquet has had its day. When American President George W. Bush visited Beijing in February 2002, Western rather than Chinese food was served at the welcoming banquet. In another break with tradition, as the banquet came to an end, in place of the usual hasty farewells an accordionist appeared, and Bush's host, President Jiang Zemin, serenaded the Americans with "*O sole mio.*"

# chapter nine

# BUSINESS BRIEFING

## CHINA'S ENTRY TO THE WORLD TRADE ORGANIZATION

China's entry to the World Trade Organization (WTO) is a highly significant event in her long history. The WTO is the only global international organization dealing with the rules of trade between nations: it is a forum in which the one-hundred-forty-plus member states can negotiate trade relations and terms. At its heart are the WTO agreements, negotiated and signed by the majority of the world's trading nations and ratified in their parliaments. The WTO's predecessor, the General Agreement on Tariffs and Trade (GATT), was a provisional organization established in 1947. In 1994 the GATT was turned into the permanent WTO.

The WTO aims at reducing tariffs and nontariff trade barriers (such as quotas) between member states. In order to do this, a member state must treat the goods and investments coming from other member states on the same terms as its own, and the rights enjoyed by one member state must be extended to all other member states.

China was one of the twenty-three original signatories of the GATT in 1948. After the revolution in 1949, the Nationalist government in Taiwan announced that China would leave the GATT system. Although the Beijing government never recognized this decision, nearly forty years later, in 1986, it notified the GATT of its wish to resume its status as a GATT contracting party.

WTO membership will require China to cease the granting of zone-based or industry-based concessions to foreign enterprises. From now on foreign investors and businesses will be making decisions based on straightforward cost rather than on policy considerations. They will be taking into account factors such as tax, land use fees, labor, corporate insurance, and employee insurance. The logistics of distribution in China means that they may find it more efficient to set up distribution, or even production, centers in the major cities. Alternatively, they could use franchising to establish themselves in the market.

Reversing the tradition of decades of employing Party members whose knowledge of (and interest in) the outside world was sketchy to say the least, China is planning to give its civil servants and those working in enterprise ("enterprise executives") special training on WTO rules. And, rather reluctantly, thousands of officials in their fifties and sixties are starting to learn English, as the government feels they should be capable of handling the expected vast increase in international communications.

For the member states of the WTO, China offers a huge potential market for investment and sales. But what does China get out of it? China's reasons for joining are to enable it to enjoy the various rights available to other member states, and to have a say on international trade matters. Some economists predict that in the short run, with the expected surge of imports and increased competition, inefficient domestic enterprises will be forced to reform or shut down, which may lead to higher unemployment. However, in the long run, there is predicted to be increased productivity, increased inflow of foreign capital, and increased transfer of technology and expertise. The official view was given in a speech in 2001 by China's President Jiang Zemin, who said that joining the WTO "is a strategic decision made by the Chinese Government under economic globalization and is in line with China's reform and opening-up policy and the goal of establishing a socialist market economic system. The efforts made by China for its WTO accession have greatly accelerated the reform and opening-up process in China."

## THE BUSINESS CULTURE

These days, there is a new confidence and pride in China, and Westerners should be very careful not to behave in a superior manner, or expect to rush things through. Things in China will proceed at the pace they wish them to—which is usually quite slow. Those Chinese who deal with foreigners are very aware of China's attraction for potential business partners, but they are also very knowledgeable about technology, international pricing, and world markets. It would be a serious mistake to treat them as some sort of "poor relation."

### Seniority Counts

The Chinese are very status conscious, so it is best to remember, when dealing with a group, that they will come into the room in order of seniority. However, the actual negotiations may be carried out by someone other than the most senior member. This may be because the most senior person is a more of a figurehead, whereas someone more junior may well have studied abroad and received an MBA at an American or other foreign university.

### Greeting People

Make sure to shake hands with everyone in the group—it is impolite to shake hands with only the first few and then give up. You will no doubt notice that there is no custom of giving precedence to the female members of the group. The Chinese incline their heads a little on meeting someone new, but there is none of the elaborate bowing that characterizes Japanese culture.

### Business Cards

When you go to a business meeting, the first thing that happens is an exchange of business cards. When someone hands you his card, make sure to read it, not just glance at it and put it away. You may well find it helpful to place the cards you receive on the table in front of you, to remind yourself of the names and titles of your Chinese counterparts.

It is a good idea to take along a large stock of business cards, if possible with a Chinese version of your name, your company's name, and your job title on the back. (See the section on names, page 73.) If you cannot get the cards made locally (for instance, through an airline or translation agency), you can probably have them printed in your own local "Chinatown," or else in Hong Kong if you are passing through; or after you get to China you can ask the reception desk in your hotel for help in finding a reliable printer. You should also take with you an indexed cardholder of some sort to keep the cards organized, as you will collect a great many of them.

Whoever chooses your Chinese name should keep it to two or three syllables—anything longer could be difficult for the Chinese to manage. And remember that the simplified forms of the Chinese characters that are now in use in the PRC are not used in Taiwan or Hong Kong. Check this when you order your cards from the printer.

## What to Wear

Dress should be quite formal. For men, suits and ties are best, with lightweight ones for the hotter, southern parts of China, or summer in the north.

It is quite acceptable for women to wear trousers, as most Chinese women do, but skirts or suits are widely perceived as smarter. Bare legs, even on the hottest summer day, are out for women. They should dress modestly (no sun-dresses or low necklines, for example), and should not behave in too extroverted a manner. "Loud" behavior or attention-seeking in either sex does not go over well in China. Banquets may call for slightly more formal wear, so take something extra smart. After years of dressing down, younger Chinese women in particular are enjoying dressing up again, often in traditional Chinese clothes made in bright colors with much embroidery. Older women (thirty-five plus) tend to dress more soberly and to shun bright colors in favor of darker ones.

### Be on Time

Punctuality is considered very important when doing business in China. The people with whom you are dealing will not keep you waiting, and you should make a point of being on time too. Equally, it is important that you should not keep looking at your watch and implying that you are in a great hurry to finish a deal. Remember, most of China works a six-day week, although some offices close on Saturday afternoons.

### Your Hosts

After your arrival in China, any arrangements for your travel within the country will usually be taken care of by the organization you are visiting. You will probably be met by representatives of the organization when you arrive, whether at the airport or the railway station, and you will also probably be seen off by them when you leave. More senior members of the organization are likely to say good-bye to you at your hotel, while relatively junior members will escort you all the way to your point of departure. This is the custom in China, and not a mark of any special esteem.

**Women in Business**

Foreign businesswomen visiting China will have no occasion to feel ill at ease simply because they are female. There may not be equal numbers of men and women in all occupations or at all levels in China, but there are, in theory at any rate, equal opportunities for both sexes, and the Chinese are quite happy to deal with both men and women, in business or as tourists.

Women who frequently visit the PRC on business report that they are well accepted by their male Chinese counterparts, and that it is not considered odd if they reciprocate toasts at banquets and so on.

Although most business entertaining is done in restaurants, it is not usual for spouses to be invited along. If your spouse is in China with you, she/he can expect to have to amuse herself/himself on the evenings when there are banquets and so on, unless specifically included in the invitation.

## CONTACTING PEOPLE

Everyone you are likely to need to contact is almost bound to have access to e-mail now. This has revolutionized the possibilities for doing business with China. The time difference with the USA, Europe, and Australia meant that phoning China was always very difficult, expensive, and unsatisfying. E-mails also fit better with the Chinese style of negotiating, as an e-mail allows someone time to reflect before they answer. It also means that individuals are more empowered than they were, now that many employees have PCs and are free to correspond directly with their Western contacts rather than go through layers of bureaucracy. (Getting to the right person initially may still take a while, but once you have your contact, things are much quicker.)

The mobile phone is another extraordinary success story in China. Only a decade or so ago, it was easier and quicker to take a taxi across Beijing or Shanghai than to get through to someone on the telephone. The Chinese shared phones—the residents of a whole apartment block could have one telephone between them, and getting though to the person you wanted could take ages. At work, people tended to use the office phone to make all the calls they couldn't make from home—so no one could ever get through to workplaces either. Telephone directories were almost unknown (as were street maps); all of this was a combination of the obsession with secrecy that characterized the 1960s and 1970s, and lack of investment in a modern telecommunications infrastructure. But Western telecommunications companies such as Cable and Wireless and Motorola that have been investing heavily in China have had a huge impact, and the Chinese are making up for lost time by talking incessantly everywhere they go on their mobile phones (the latest models), and sending hundreds of millions of text messages. It is another huge step on the path of modernization, with the government proving that it now trusts its people and knows how vital rapid communications are in the twenty-first century.


## NEGOTIATING TECHNIQUES

### Help is at Hand

There are many sources of help for businesses that want to set up in China. Consultancies are a popular route. There are government-sponsored business promotion bodies in most countries, and they usually have offices in China. Chinese organizations are very good at PR these days, and will often have a website and literature, but they should be carefully and independently appraised (by the Chamber of Commerce or the relevant trade association). There are literally thousands of useful websites about China; look for ones that are run out of the USA or Hong Kong, as they tend to be less starry-eyed. Do not rush into China; costs are high and it is easy to be fooled by all the hype about the "world's biggest market."

### When "No" Means "Maybe"

When engaged in business dealings, as in other situations, a Chinese person may feel that a direct "no" would be embarrassing to both parties, and try to convey his disagreement by more indirect methods, such as evading the question or remaining silent. The Western business person will need to be sensitive to this, and learn to interpret the signals that his or her Chinese counterpart is giving out. In some cases, of course, what appears to be an attempt at stalling may genuinely mean that the person you are dealing with has to consult his superiors, but in other cases it may be a sign that concessions on your part are required if the discussions are to go much further.

Requests for "commissions" and other forms of under-the-table payments are common, especially in the more anarchistic south of the country. They are likely to be made indirectly. If the request is direct, rejection can be phrased in terms of "My country makes such payments illegal and my company would be in big trouble if it . . . "

## Acceptable Outcomes

Westerners tend to expect results from meetings. The results may be an action plan, an agreement to meet again, or a decision, and minutes of the meeting are taken to provide a record of what is said. Chinese meetings are less likely to lead to a result, at least not so quickly. They are an opportunity for people to state a position, which they will have decided in advance. There is rarely an agenda. There is a strict observance of rank as to who actually does the talking, and interrupting is considered rude. In the more modern, go-ahead companies things are changing fast, and meetings will resemble the free-for-all, give and take, that Westerners are used to. But officialdom in China is slow to change and so are the longer-established organizations.

## Preparation

If you prepare properly and well in advance for a meeting in China, it will work better for all concerned. Paperwork about your company, your plans, and your project will have been read and discussed with a care and thoughtfulness that many Western managers can only dream of! It is better to come with a clear set of objectives, which each side has had time to think about, than to use the meeting as a sort of brainstorming session in the way that Westerners tend to.

# Listening and Presentation Styles

Here is a summary of the different cultural expectations each side brings to the relationship.

| USE OF NAME | **Western:** Tend to use first names on first meeting. |
| | **Chinese:** More formal; use titles such as Mr. or Miss, or Mayor, Manager, Professor. |
| USE OF HUMOR | **Western:** Tell jokes and use humor as an icebreaker |
| | **Chinese:** Very sparing use of humor on first meeting—except for a carefully planned joke. But this is changing. |
| INTERRUPTIONS | **Western:** Feel free to interrupt the speaker and put their own point of view. Colleagues are geared up to respond to the body language of the person who wants to interrupt. |
| | **Chinese:** Interrupting would be rude. But people take endless calls on their cell phones! Staff often pop in and whisper messages to senior executives. It is not rude to whisper to a colleague while someone else is speaking. |
| MAKING SURE YOU ARE UNDERSTOOD | **Western:** It is usual to structure presentations and to recap what has been said. It is normal for to ask for clarification if necessary. The speaker is to blame if something is not as clear as it should be. |
| | **Chinese:** Being clearly understood is not a priority, perhaps because at school they are used to listening in silence to the teacher. Saying "I don't understand" is a possible loss of face. |
| ARGUMENT VS. AGREEMENT | **Western:** People expect to argue things through and enjoy doing so. It is not rude to be adversarial. This is often the way to get noticed and promoted. |

| | |
|---|---|
| | **Chinese:** The Chinese can be very argumentative, but this is unlikely to be displayed in front of a foreigner, even when they know and trust him or her. |
| **ATTENTION SPAN** | **Western:** Short, and getting shorter. Westerners tend to assume that people will be bored and try to come to the point quickly. |
| | **Chinese:** Longer. The Chinese are trained from early childhood to listen politely and patiently. They do not come to the point quickly—to do so would be rude. You may not hear the information you have been waiting for until the meeting is almost over. |
| **EYE CONTACT** | **Western:** Too much eye contact makes people uneasy. Too little and they distrust you. |
| | **Chinese:** Keep eye contact with your interlocutor. People who avoid eye contact are not considered trustworthy. |
| **PRAISE** | **Western:** Politeness and praise are important, but too much is seen as flattery and is mistrusted. |
| | **Chinese:** Flattery is part of the negotiating process. It is given by praising people in front of their peers, and by expressing deference to superiors. |
| **SELF-DEPRECATION** | **Western:** In Britain this is used a lot, less so in the U.S.A. |
| | **Chinese:** Individuals rarely criticize themselves, but will criticize their organization, or China. |
| **GETTING THINGS DONE** | **Western:** Orders and instructions, even if given in a friendly manner, are direct. They can be questioned. |
| | **Chinese:** Orders are given more indirectly, but compliance is expected. Instructions may be vague (this is a safety net), but carry authority. |

**Final Decisions May Not Be Final**
Be prepared for the Chinese side to request changes
to a contract even after it has been signed. Long-
term relationships are more important than quick
deals. It can take a long time for a contract to be
signed. If you can get it translated into Chinese at
your end, this will speed things up a bit.

## WORKING HOURS AND VACATIONS

The Chinese get to work very early, but are not the
most efficient users of time. They have a saying: "In
the West, you waste everything except time; in China
[where everything is recycled] we waste nothing
except time." There are usually too many people in
offices, shops, and factories, and people often do not
have enough to do. Regular meal breaks punctuate
the day—lunch is early, often at 12 noon, and in the
hot weather many will take a siesta after lunch (the
word is *xiuxi*, meaning rest). People go home around
4:00 or 5:00 p.m., and working late is rare, especially
as public transport and roads are crowded and
people have long, tiring journeys home.

In the days of Mao, holidays were almost
unknown. Nowadays, paid holidays are becoming
more widespread, especially at Chinese New Year
(February), Labor Day (May 1), and National Day
(October 1). A week off for one or all of these
national holidays is intended to encourage the

Chinese, by nature used to saving their money, to go out and get the economy moving by spending it in the shops and restaurants (and perhaps to feel that these patriotic days are more fun than they used to be). It seems to have been a pretty successful move.

Academic holidays are similar to those in the West, with the notable exception that there is no Christmas break. The school year begins in September. Students have their winter holidays from mid-January to the end of February, and their summer holidays from mid-July to the end of August. The dates of the winter holiday are set each year, as the Spring Festival is not fixed.

As we have seen, punctuality is important. However, once you have arrived, there is less of a rush than in the frantically busy West.

Working patterns differ from the West; for example, Western film producers who are used to their film crews working a ten-hour day when making a TV program find that the Chinese crews put in about five hours a day by the time lunch and various rest periods are taken into account. On the other hand, discuss and negotiate with your Chinese partners; if they know what you expect and need from them they will always try to accommodate you. Ironically there are no trade union regulations in China; health and safety rules are very lax, and, for better or for worse, each contract is more or less up to the individual organizations involved.

# chapter ten

# COMMUNICATING

## MANDARIN, CANTONESE, AND OTHER FORMS OF CHINESE

Because of China's geography, transport and communications have always been difficult, so it is not surprising that over the course of her history, several different forms of the Chinese language have developed. These are usually referred to as "dialects," but since they are in many cases mutually unintelligible, it is more helpful to think of them as separate languages. There are eight major dialects, including Mandarin, Cantonese, Shanghai, Hakka, Amoy, Fuzhou, and Wenzhou, and many minor regional variations.

Mandarin is the official language used in both the PRC and Taiwan as the medium of education, and is the common means of communication in China. In the PRC it is called *putonghua* (common or standard speech), as well as *hanyu* (the language of the *han* people) and *zhongwen* (Chinese). In Taiwan it is known as *guoyu* (national language) or *huayu*. In theory, anyone under about fifty-five should be able to speak Mandarin—even if they prefer to speak their own local variety of Chinese at home—but in practice this is not always the case.

Chinese is a tone-language, part of the Sino-Tibetan family of languages. English, by contrast, belongs to the Indo-European family. There are other south Asian languages that work in the same way as Chinese: Vietnamese, Burmese, and Thai, for example. Tone languages are those in which a variation in the pitch of the voice in which a particular syllable is pronounced conveys differences in meaning. For example, *tang* said in a high level tone means "soup," but *tang* said in a rising tone means "sugar"; *gou* said in a fall-rise tone means "dog," but *gou* said with a falling tone means "enough."

There are four tones in Mandarin:

> level (and relatively high)
> rising
> fall-rise
> falling

This may sound complicated, but compared to other dialects—for example, Cantonese, which may have up to nine tones—it is fairly simple. For most non-Chinese-speaking people the tones are the greatest obstacle to speaking Chinese correctly. Foreigners are often described as tone deaf, as they have trouble even hearing the different tones, never mind reproducing them. They need a good deal of practice but, as with using chopsticks, if you ask your Chinese contacts to help you improve your pronunciation, this can be a useful conversational gambit. You still won't get it right, but your hosts can have a lot of fun helping you. Do not despair, however. As with any language, learning does *not* consist of repeating isolated words devoid of context. Learning some simple phrases is quite easy. Any minor difficulty you may have in learning these phrases will be far outweighed by the positive reaction you will get from Chinese people, and the context, as well as the willingness of your hosts to try and respond to your efforts, will help understanding.

Most Chinese words are made up of one syllable. Each syllable is represented by a single Chinese character. Chinese has fewer sounds than some other languages; as English has more sounds, there are very few actual Chinese sounds (as opposed to tones) that pose problems for English speakers.

**Understanding Chinese English**
The same is not true the other way around. According to the Chinese writer Jung Chang: "In general, Chinese speakers find English hard to pronounce and have trouble learning to

understand the spoken language." She points out how one of the features that English speakers notice about the Chinese is the difficulty they have with what linguists call "reduced syllables." Chinese speakers tend to stress too many syllables. For example, they find it hard to say, as an English speaker would, "fish'n'chips," and will either say "fish-and-chips," or just "fish chips." The Chinese tend to separate the syllables of English words, and also the words themselves, as they would in Chinese. This leads to a sort of machine-gun effect when they speak English (especially for Cantonese speakers), rather than the smooth but varied "stream" effect that English should give. Combined with the fact that "please," "thank you," and "sorry" are not used nearly as often in Chinese as in English, this may lead to a perception of rudeness.

Another problem for speakers of some Chinese dialects (not Mandarin) is the lack of the sounds "r" and "n." So the phrase: "*Ni shi nei guo ren?*" or "What country are you from?" would be pronounced "*Li shi leiguo len*?" with the sound "l" substituted for both the initial "n" and "r." This is what led to the old caricatures of the Chinese saying things like "flied lice" instead of "fried rice" when Chinese people started to come to the USA and Europe at the beginning of the last century.

### Pidgin English

The word "pidgin" (pronounced "pigeon," like the bird) comes from early Chinese attempts to pronounce the word "business." When traders from the USA, Britain, and Portugal visited the coasts of China in the early 1800s they found that understanding each other's language was a long and tedious process. Pidgin English, consisting of a few hundred English words, grew up as a way of filling this linguistic vacuum. The words were not used grammatically, and they popped up in Chinese sentence structures with Chinese pronunciation. The blend was made richer by the addition of some words of Hindi and Urdu, brought over by traders who had worked with the East India Company. After the Communists gained power in 1949 pidgin died out as it carried too much of the baggage of colonialism, but until then it was not only used as a way for foreigners and Chinese to communicate, but also for speakers of different Chinese dialects to talk to each other, before *putonghua* took over that role.

Picturesque words from those days survive in a few comic book stories such as *TinTin*, words like "*chop chop*," meaning hurry up. "*Chop*" on its own meant a trademark, brand, or name. Another one which survives is "*joss*" (as in joss-stick, a stick of incense), which comes from the Portuguese word "*deos*" (God), and means idol, god, or luck; from this comes the wonderful "*joss-pidgin-man*," or "god business man"—better known as a priest.

## PINYIN: THE ROMANIZATION OF CHINESE CHARACTERS

The system of transliteration used in this book, Pinyin, was adopted by the PRC in 1979. The system it has replaced was called Wade-Giles, named after its inventors. This is why it is often confusing to read books written some years ago with differently Romanized versions of Chinese place-names, such as Soochow, now written Suzhou. Add to that differences in regional accents, changes in place-names over time, and the Chinese habit of giving Chinese place-names to everywhere (such as Kashi for the northwestern town of Kashgar), and it is a wonder anyone gets anywhere. There are also places in the south of China that Westerners call by a version of their Cantonese name—such as Hong Kong—that the Mandarin speakers who make up most of China (about 70 percent) call by their Mandarin name, in this case Xiang Gang ("Fragrant Harbor").

Nevertheless, the standardization that Pinyin has provided for the Chinese language is immensely useful. For example, telephone directories and dictionaries use it—since Chinese does not have an alphabet as such, this is the only way to order the information. Computer keyboards use Pinyin. For example, if you type in the word *ma*, using the two letters of our alphabet *m* and *a*, the screen gives you a choice of the many different Chinese characters that can be used to write the word, depending on its meaning. You just click on the correct character.

### The Sounds of Pinyin

Foreign learners should remember that they cannot automatically give the letters their usual sounds. Many of the sounds in Chinese do approximate to English sounds, but there are a number of conventions that have to be observed.

- c is pronounced as *ts* in "cats"
- z is pronounced as *ds* in "seeds"
- q is pronounced as *ch* in "cheap"
- j is pronounced as *j* in "jig"
- x is pronounced as something between *sh* in "shin" and *s*
- s as in "siesta"
- r is pronounced as a cross between *s* in "vision" and *r* in "red"
- h is pronounced as *ch* in Scottish "loch"
- zh is pronounced as *j* in "July"
- a is like *ar* in "far"

- **-ang** is like *ung* in Southern English "sung"
- **e** is like *er* in "her"
- **en** is like *en* in "stricken"
- **ei** is like *ay* in "hay"
- **ou** is like *ou* in "soul"
- **i** is like *ee* in "see," except after **c**, **s**, **z**, **r**, **ch**, **sh**, and **zh**, when it is like the *i* in American "sir"
- **u** is like *oo* in "soon"
- **ï** is like *e* in "see" but said with the lips rounded as if for "oo"
- **-ong** is like *ung* in German "Jung"
- **-ian** is like "yen"
- **ui** is like "way"

## WRITTEN CHINESE

Believed to be among the world's oldest written languages, early Chinese writing was based on pictograms that evolved into characters formed by a series of brushstrokes. Some Chinese characters can be traced back to their origins as simple pictures of the things they represent. Sun (*taiyang*) was a circle with a dot in the middle; now it is written like a box with a line across it. Water (*shui*) is three flowing lines; a person (*ren*) looks like a little (headless) human with two legs. These simple concepts can be combined to make new ones; the characters for sun and moon together make the character for "bright." The character for "family" is made by putting "roof" over "pig."

Written Chinese is largely uniform throughout the country, although many of the characters are now written in a simplified form. In Hong Kong (for the time being) and Taiwan and other overseas Chinese communities the older, more complex form of the Chinese characters is used.

Estimates of the number of characters vary— but there are probably about 50,000. A working knowledge of a mere 3,000 gives you mastery of most menus and street signs; if you want to read the newspapers you will need about 7,000.

Most Chinese characters consist of two parts: the radical, which shows to which class the word belongs, and the phonetic, which tells how it is pronounced. For example, the character for pure, or clear, *qing*, has two parts; the water radical and the part which gives the pronunciation, *qing*.

清　氵　water radical (word category)

青　phonetic element (pronunciation)

There are about 250 radicals, some quite common, such as the one used for anything concerned with fire, others more unusual.

Although learning Chinese characters appears a nightmarish task to Westerners , Chinese children start young and work very hard at it; illiteracy is low, though of course the number of characters a person knows depends on their educational level and on their job. The Chinese find the alphabetic script of Western languages difficult to decode: "…the way the information is spread out in each word seems cumbersome for a reader used to the compact ideograms of Chinese," as Jung Chang puts it.

One of the problems with each character being different (although the radicals give a clue, they can have a fairly loose connection with the actual meaning of the word) is that it is possible for the Chinese to come across a word they have never seen before in the newspapers or a book and not to know how to pronounce it. Another example of this was the occasion when a foreign teacher in Beijing wanted to buy a dice (or die) for her students to play board games with in lessons. Not surprisingly, given the Chinese love of gambling, everyone knew the word for this object, but no one knew how to write it down so that the teacher could show it to the shop assistants (possibly because under Mao gambling had been forbidden for decades). Eventually a very old man was found who knew how to write it—it turned out to have a bone radical, as in the days before plastic that was what dice were made of—but even when he wrote the character down, none of the young shop assistants could read it!

For foreigners, knowledge of a few Chinese characters is useful (exit, entrance, and so on) but not as necessary as knowledge of the spoken language. If desired though, the study of Chinese can become a lifelong interest.

## CALLIGRAPHY

Chinese people love to hang calligraphy on their walls—exquisitely painted Chinese characters that are either famous poems, mostly from the Tang dynasty, or well-known sayings. The art of the calligrapher is as appreciated as the art of the painter, and people can recognize who has written/painted the characters in the same way that a Westerner can spot a Picasso or a Monet painting. Because characters are considered lovely in themselves, over the centuries many famous Chinese paintings and scrolls have had beautifully penned characters added to them by famous artists, usually expressing their appreciation of the picture. These are thought to add to their value. There is no Western equivalent to this—it would be as though a painting by Rembrandt had messages of critical acclaim from Cezanne and other painters scribbled down the side, which added another million dollars or two to its value at auction.

Another great difference is that where Western art and indeed most cultures prize originality above everything (sometimes seemingly above the actual quality of the art), Chinese art for centuries stuck firmly to the Confucian principle of constantly recreating the golden age of the past; techniques were learned (and still are) so that the pupil could paint in exactly the same way that the masters had painted several hundred years before he was born—and the subjects (bamboo, plum blossom, and so on) also never changed. Young Chinese painters are breaking away from this tradition; Chen Zhi Li, China's first-ever female minister of education, has been eloquent on the importance of changing the school system to encourage children to be more creative. As it looks forward to the challenges of the twenty-first century, China's latest slogan—perhaps mission statement would be a more appropriate term nowadays—is a newly articulated desire to "emancipate the mind and march with time."

culture smart! china

# Appendix: Simple Vocabulary

**Ni hao?**
Hello (lit., you well?)

**Zaijian**
Good-bye (lit., again see)

**Xie xie**
Thank you

**Bu keqi**
You're welcome (in reply to thank you)

**Duibuqi**
Sorry, excuse me (not used as much as in English)

**Duile**
Yes (lit., correct)

**Shi de**
Yes (lit., it is so)

**Bu shi**
No (lit., it is not so)

**Qing zuo**
Please be seated

**Qing gei wo**
Please give me

**Qing jin**
Please come in

**Yingguo**
England

**Yingguoren**
Englishman/woman

**Yingyu**
English (language)

**Meiguo**
America

**Meiguoren**
American man/woman

**Zhongguo**
China

**Zhonguoren**
Chinese man/woman

**Hanyu (in the PRC)**
Chinese (language)

**Jianada**
Canada

**Jianadaren**
Canadian

**Aodaliya**
Australia

**Aodilayaren**
Australian man/woman

**Wo bu hui shuo hanyu**
I can't speak Chinese

**Wo shi**
I am...

**Zai nar**
Where is...?

**Sanguan**
Restaurant

**Fandian**
Hotel

**Cesuo**
Toilet

**Huochizhan**
Railway station

**Ziyou shichang**
Market

### Note

There are no direct equivalents for "Yes," "No," or "Please." For "Yes" you could use *duile*, which really means "correct"; or you can say, *shi de*, which means, "it is so." Instead of "No," you could sometimes use *bu shi*. As for "Please," you will hear Chinese people using *qing* followed by a verb, but this literally means "I invite you to…" For example, you can say *qing gei wo* (please give me), or *qing jin* (please come in).

# Further Reading

## Guide Books

Crowe, Carl. *The Handbook for China*. Oxford: Oxford Paperbacks, 1986.

Harper, Damien, et al. *Lonely Planet: China*. Melbourne/Oakland/London/Paris: Lonely Planet Publications, 2002.

Leffman, David, et al. *The Rough Guide to China*. London: Rough Guides, 2000.

Sinclair, Kevin and Iris Wong Po-yee. *Culture Shock! China: A Guide to Customs and Etiquette*. Portland, Oregon: Graphic Arts Center Publishing, 2001/London: Kuperard, 2003.

## Phrase Books

Flower, Kathy. *Get by in Mandarin*. London: BBC Worldwide, 1998.

Qian, Lin (ed.). *Everyday Chinese*. London: Kuperard, 1992.

*Ultimate Mandarin Chinese Course*. New York: Living Language, 1998.

## Cookery

Hom, Ken. *A Taste of China*. London: Pavilion Books, 1990.

## History and Politics

Becker, Jasper. 1. *The Chinese*. 2. *Hungry Ghosts*. London: John Murray, 1996.

Benewick, R. *China in the 1990s*. London: Macmillan, 1999.

Cotterell, A. *China, A History*. London: Random House, 1995.

Murray, M.G. *China The Next Superpower. Dilemmas in Change and Continuity*. China Library, 1998.

Owen, S. *An Anthology of Chinese Literature*. London: W.W. Norton, 1997.

Spence, Jonathan D. *The Gate of Heavenly Peace: The Chinese and Their Revolution 1895-1980*. London: Faber & Faber, 1982.

Thubron, Colin. *Behind the Wall*. London: Heinemann, 1987.

Wright, Elizabeth. *The Chinese People Stand Up*. London: BBC Books, 1989.

## Business

*Chinese Business Companion. The Language Guide for Business*. New York: Living Language, 1998.

Blackman, Carolyn. *Negotiating China: Case Studies and Strategies*. 1. *Operating in China*. 2. *Business China*. London: Economist Intelligence Unit, 1998.

Luah, Larry T. L. *Success Secrets to Maximize Business in China*. Singapore/Kuala Lumpur: Times Books International, 2001.

Stross, Randall E. *Bulls in the China Shop, and other Sino-American Business Encounters*. New York: Pantheon Books, 1991.

## Autobiography

Binyan, Liu. *A Higher Kind of Loyalty*. New York: Random House, 1990.

Chang, Jung. *Wild Swans*. London: Flamingo, 1993.

Ye, Ting-xing. *A Leaf in the Bitter Wind*. London: Bantam Books, 2000.

culture smart! china

# Index

culture smart! china